Get a Faith Lift!

Reshape Your Outlook with Guidance from God

NELL WEBB MOHNEY

DIMENSIONS
FOR LIVING
NASHVILLE

GET A FAITH LIFT!
Reshape Your Outlook with Guidance from God

Copyright © 2000 by Dimensions for Living

This book is printed on acid-free paper.

Library of Congress Cataloging-in-Publication Data

Mohney, Nell.
  Get a faith lift! : reshape your outlook with guidance from God / Nell Webb Mohney.
    p. cm.
  ISBN 0-687-09016-4 (alk. paper)
    1. Christian life.   I. Title.

BV4501.2 .M547 2000
242—dc21   99-054020

00 01 02 03 04 05 06 07 08 09—10 9 8 7 6 5 4 3 2

MANUFACTURED IN THE UNITED STATES OF AMERICA

To

my husband and best friend, Dr. Ralph W. Mohney,

without whom this book would not be possible.

He has encouraged my writing;

stimulated and challenged my thinking;

served as wise counselor and revisionist editor;

and told me funny stories when I was weary.

Acknowledgments

I express grateful appreciation to:

Sally Sharpe, my knowledgeable and able editor and close personal friend, for her work on this project;

Helen Exum, former executive vice president of the *Chattanooga Free Press* in Chattanooga, Tennessee, for allowing me to draw most of the material for this book from articles I wrote for that paper;

and the personnel of the Reference Department of the Hamilton County Bicentennial Public Library, for their willing and endless research at my request.

Contents

Introduction

We live in a time of tremendous change. It is a time of great challenges as well as incredible opportunities. One of the most important ways we can prepare ourselves to meet these challenges and opportunities successfully is to get a faith lift. That's right: a *faith* lift! I am convinced that God needs to be shaping a new you and a new me in this new era. The challenges and opportunities are so great that we can't just do "business as usual." In order to fulfill God's eternal purposes, we must allow God to shape us more and more into the likeness of Christ (2 Corinthians 4:10). As the apostle Paul says, "We have this treasure in earthen vessels" (2 Corinthians 4:7 KJV). It is our earthen vessels that need reshaping. So we must be malleable, and remember that even the earthen vessels that have been broken or badly marred can be made beautiful by God.

The eighteenth chapter of Jeremiah tells of going to the potter's house. The potter is shaping a vessel, and it is badly marred. Yet he doesn't throw it away but reshapes it into a thing of beauty. This can be true of us as well. God, the Great Potter, never discards us; whatever our past, God can make us anew if we are willing. Isaiah 43:19 reminds us: "[Behold], I am doing a new thing! [Lo], it springs up; do you not perceive it?" (NIV).

The chapters of this book explore areas of our lives and our outlooks that may need reshaping if we are to be God's instruments, splendidly ready for the new millennium. Because some of these areas overlap at times, and because there are key Christian principles and practices that apply to more than one area, you will note that some points are repeated as necessary and appropriate throughout the book. The main points or "steps" pertaining to each area of discussion are also repeated at the end of each chapter for quick and easy reference, making the book a ready resource for anytime you may need inspiration, motivation, or guidance. Repetition not only helps to reinforce ideas and concepts but also gives emphasis and clarity to some of the "unshakable certainties" of the Christian faith and life. An added benefit is that you may read through the entire book or, if you prefer, you may pick and choose chapters that speak to specific areas or needs of your life *right now*. However you use the book, my prayer is that you may be willing to examine your life under God's microscope and then allow God to reshape you. *May your shaping in the Potter's hand be for gladness!*

Chapter 1

Get a Faith Lift

I pray that, according to the riches of his glory, he may
grant that you may be strengthened in your inner being
with power through his Spirit.

—Ephesians 3:16

One day at the airport I ran into a friend I hadn't
seen for years. She looked gorgeous. Since we both
were hurrying to catch planes and didn't have time to
talk, I blurted out the words that immediately came to
mind when I saw her: "Have you had a face lift? You
look wonderful!" Since her plane was being called, she
replied as she ran, "Not a face lift, but a *faith* lift!"

Instantly I thought of another time when I heard
those exact words. It was in 1981, during an interview
with the talented and vivacious country music star Jan
Howard, whose life had been riddled by tragedy.

Jan married at age sixteen and had three children, a
nervous breakdown, and a divorce by the time she was
twenty. Unfortunately, she had no deep resources of
faith to sustain her. As a child growing up in West
Plains, Missouri, she had witnessed a "hell fire and
damnation" revival which had terrified her. "I knew
many religious fanatics who not only frightened me, but
who pushed me away from faith," she told me.

In 1957, when her oldest son was nine, Jan married

Harlan Howard, a songwriter living in Los Angeles, California. Soon thereafter, Harlan heard her singing in the shower and persuaded her to sing for one of his demo records. Never having sung publicly, Jan was hesitant. But she did it, and she liked it—and so did the producers. She achieved stardom without even seeking it. In 1959, her record "The One You Slip Around With" became one of the top ten country music records. Her first road show quickly followed, including a performance on the Johnny Horton, Archie Campbell Show.

In 1960, when the Howards moved to Nashville, Jan decided to start going to church "for the boys' sake." The boys became active in church, and each was baptized in the Christian faith. Though Jan attended church with them, she did not think that a personal commitment to Christ was a viable option for her. Actually, she felt no need for it. She was doing quite well on her own.

Then it happened! Life began to come apart at the seams. First, her oldest son, Jimmy, was drafted in the Vietnam War. When she put him on the plane, she had an intuitive feeling that she would never see him alive again. That feeling was prophetic. On October 30, 1968, Jimmy, age twenty-one, was killed in action. His next oldest brother, Carter, who by that time also was serving in Vietnam, brought his brother's body home.

For Jan, Jimmy's death was devastating. It was something she couldn't accept, yet she was powerless to change it. *Where was God?* she wondered. *How could God allow such suffering?* In her pain, she withdrew from everything and even stopped singing for a while. Perhaps it was the memory of Jimmy's request—"Mom, keep on singing the song 'When No One Stands Alone' for me"—that started her singing again.

Yet the trail of tears had not ended for Jan Howard. Her youngest son, David, enveloped by grief at the needless death of his brother, suffered a nervous breakdown and later got into the drug scene. In 1973, at age twenty-one, David took his own life. That was when Jan experienced the lowest depths of despair. Simply functioning was too painful for her. In effect, she dropped out of life for two years.

Then, in 1978, she took a trip to the Holy Land. In describing the experience, she said, "If you are an atheist, there is no way to stay one as you retrace the footsteps of Jesus." On the anniversary of Jimmy's death, she was standing on the balcony of her hotel room in Tiberias, overlooking the Sea of Galilee. Her unspoken prayer was, "Lord, if you will just ease this burden and take away some of the grief, I will release my sons to you." God did, and she did. She was baptized in the river Jordan. Since that time she has made a serious and systematic study of the scriptures and has had some exciting opportunities for growth in faith.

Just the week before I talked with her, she had an unusual experience of God's direction. While singing for a benefit in Washington, D.C., to raise money for the Vietnam veterans, she received word that her twenty-six-year-old nephew had been killed in an automobile accident. She flew to Los Angeles to be with her brother, a widower, whose whole life was centered on this only child. Her brother was not a man of faith. There was no mention of God in the funeral service. The body was cremated; and since both father and son were sky divers, the father planned to drive one hundred miles into the desert, go up in a plane, and parachute out to sprinkle the ashes of his son's body on the hot desert sands. The night before, he confided to Jan in bitterness and despair that he would not pull the ripcord and would join his son in death.

Her brother would not allow Jan to speak of her faith,

but he couldn't keep her from praying, "Lord, please don't let him go up in that plane." The next day she drove with him and a friend to the desert. When they approached the plane, her brother turned to Jan and said, "I'm not going up in that plane." It was clearly an answer to prayer and the first step toward being able to share with her brother something of her own faith. She told him, "Whereas once I felt I was self-sufficient, now I know I can do nothing without the love and guidance of Christ."

As I concluded the interview that day and looked into the lovely face of Jan Howard, it was obvious to me that she truly had had a faith lift.

Steps to Getting a Faith Lift

1. Remember that you are not in charge of the universe. God is! Though God has given us minds and expects us to use our best judgment, we can't control other people or all of our circumstances.

2. Remember that Jesus gave us a three-step formula for finding or renewing faith: "Ask, and it shall be given you; seek, and ye shall find; knock and it shall be opened unto you" (Matthew 7:7 KJV).

3. Use the formula that Jesus has given you. *Ask* God to direct you onto the path of truth. Seek this truth and stay open to it through Bible study, worship, prayer, and people who will point the way. *Knock* at the door of opportunity—of service. By serving others in the name of Christ, you will find him standing in your midst.

4. Believe and receive. In Matthew 9:27-29, we find the story of two blind men who asked Jesus to

restore their sight. Jesus asked, "Do you believe that I am able to do this?" They replied, "Yes, Lord." Then Jesus restored their sight, saying, "According to your faith let it be done to you." Likewise, we need to believe and receive this gift of faith, and then live our lives in gratitude for it.

5. Remember that when we allow the living presence of Christ to live in our hearts, we are empowered to be "more than conquerors" (Romans 8:37).

Chapter 2

Believe in Yourself

[Jesus] said to him, "'You shall love the Lord your God with all your heart, and with all your soul, and with all your mind.' This is the greatest and first commandment. And a second is like it: 'You shall love your neighbor as yourself.'"

—*Matthew 22:37-39*

A new millennium needs a vast army of people who are strong in body, mind, and spirit. If we, as individuals, know who we are and to whom we belong, we can help to fulfill God's purposes in this world.

When a lawyer asked Jesus to identify the greatest commandment, Jesus replied: " 'You shall love the Lord your God with all your heart, and with all your soul, and with all your mind.' This is the greatest and first commandment. And a second is like it: 'You shall love your neighbor as yourself'" (Matthew 22:37-39). In this passage, Jesus gave us life's truly eternal triangle: love for God, love for others, and love for ourselves. In order to love ourselves, we must know ourselves (children of God, created in God's image), like ourselves, and believe in ourselves. We can do the latter because we have been redeemed by Christ and empowered by the Holy Spirit.

My day had been crowded and stressful. The dishwasher wasn't working, which meant that the simple chore of dishwashing took twice as much time. The tedious job of correcting a manuscript was lengthened by constant interruptions. The bright spot of my day was to have been watching my granddaughter, Ellen, participate in a track meet late in the afternoon. Even the excitement of that event was dampened when we had to sit huddled under umbrellas and raincoats in the driving rain. I was in no mood for an upbeat interview with speaker and best-selling author Jack Canfield. But he was expecting my call at 5:30 P.M. So, wet and hungry, I placed the call to a man whose book, *Chicken Soup for the Soul* was then number one on the *New York Times* best-seller list. In less than five minutes of conversation with this man, whose books and speeches have helped hundreds of people believe in themselves, I had forgotten my problems and felt energized enough to conquer the world!

As we talked, I learned more about this powerful motivator. In addition to being president of the Canfield Training Group in Culver City, California, and director of the Optimum Performance Training Institute in Pasadena, California, he serves as the chairman of the board of the Foundation for Self-Esteem. Perhaps it is his pioneer work related to the importance of self-esteem for which he is best known.

The basic human need for strong self-esteem became most evident to him twenty years ago when he was a teacher in an inner city school. He noticed that the children were extremely verbal on the playground but became shy and reticent in the classroom. So he began to investigate what blocks individuals from using the full potential of the human mind.

The program he developed to enable people to live happy, more fulfilling lives has been taught in varying formats to educators, Fortune 500 executives, and religious and government leaders on three continents. As we talked that day on the phone, he shared with me ten specific steps for becoming a happier, more fulfilled person. After reading his books and listening to his tapes, I am convinced that every one of us can profit from these steps that keep us continually growing and accomplishing. Here they are, along with my own parenthetical comments:

1. Move forward by completing the past. (Too often we have unfinished business with parents, siblings, or even ourselves. In order to move confidently into the future, we need time to think, talk with a friend or counselor, pray, and perhaps have a "care-frontation.")
2. Use positive self-talk to quiet the inner critics of doubt and perfectionism. (Instead of saying things like "That was dumb," "I am so stupid," or "I can't ever do anything right" when we do something poorly, we should say, "Next time, I'll do it this way." Arnold Palmer says he does this every time he makes a bad golf shot.)
3. Acknowledge your personal and professional strengths. (Too often we focus on our weaknesses and failures rather than building on our strengths.)
4. Clarify your vision of the future before attempting to get there.
5. Set specific goals and objectives. (Remember that unless they are specific, we are still in the land of wishful thinking. Only specific goals and objectives motivate us to take action.)
6. See yourself succeeding. (This is the number one secret of successful persons, including star athletes. Envision success, whether you are playing a golf game, giving a speech, or conducting a business

meeting. Afterward, affirm your success by saying something such as, "I did a good job. That was more like me.")

7. Take action—now. (Give up the "if only's" and just do it!)
8. Respond positively to feedback. (Don't be defensive, learn from the feedback. Remember, it is through constructive criticism that we can see ourselves most clearly and can grow.)
9. Persevere. (Just keep on keeping on. Don't stop short of the goal.)
10. Celebrate every success along the way.

As I talked with Jack Canfield, two things especially impressed me. One was his strong religious faith; the other was his devotion to his family. At one point in the interview I said, "You have accomplished so much in your life. What are you most proud of?" Without a moment's hesitation he replied, "Our three children." Without a doubt, Jack Canfield is the kind of person from whom we can learn a great deal. His strategies can help each of us move into the future with confidence and success!

Steps to Believing in Yourself

1. Do as Jesus taught: Love God, love yourself, and love others (see Matthew 22:37-39).
2. Follow Jack Canfield's ten strategies for confident living!

Chapter 3

Don't Linger in Self-Pity

God is faithful, and he will not let you be tested beyond your strength, but with the testing he will also provide the way out so that you may be able to endure it.

—*1 Corinthians 10:13*

*T*o move confidently into this new century, we cannot linger long in self-pity. To do so means we will be held in its clutches. Wallowing in self-pity means we become a "whiner," a constant complainer. Self-pity destroys creativity. It banishes friends and causes us to play the "blame game" instead of taking full responsibility for our lives.

I know a person who has the right to feel sorry for himself, but he doesn't. As a result, he is one of the most talented and creative musicians I know. His name is Ken Medema. He has served as organist, pianist, and music director for the International Women's Conference at the Crystal Cathedral in Garden Grove, California, many times.

Ken captures the audience with his music, most of which he composes as the conference progresses. He writes the theme song for the conference. And at the close of each speaker's address, Ken summarizes the main points through the song he composed as the speaker spoke. It is one of the most delightful and amazing feats of creativity I have ever observed.

We were days into our conference before I realized that Ken was blind. He was born blind, as was his younger sister. Both received a recessive gene which caused the blindness. They were born in Grand Rapids, Michigan, the only children of "salt of the earth" Dutch Calvinist parents from the Netherlands.

Ken told me that his parents were not well educated and had a very low income. Even so, his mother and father were wise enough to join a support group for parents of blind children. The group's leader, a psychologist, strongly advised the parents not to be overprotective of their children but to treat them as any other children. This parenting philosophy, plus the warmth of his parents' love and the absolute sincerity of their religious beliefs, seemed to liberate both Ken and his sister, enabling them to develop to their full potential.

The Medemas sensed Ken's musical ability and saved enough on their limited income to buy him a second-hand upright piano. For Ken, music was a world of excitement and joy. He spent every free minute playing the piano—even before he began taking piano lessons. When he was eight years old, his parents decided that he must have lessons. Once again, they provided the opportunity through personal sacrifice. The teacher was a talented graduate of the Julliard School of Music in New York City who had returned to Grand Rapids because of a family problem. Immediately she knew that Ken had a special gift. "She helped me to listen to all kinds of music—symphony, jazz, eastern, European," Ken recalled. "She was a soul mate, and she seemed to enjoy the newness of helping me."

Ken was in a special class in elementary school, but he learned mobility early and was able to participate in regular classes in junior and senior high. His classmates didn't harass or make fun of him; they simply ignored him. More and more he turned to music as his life. In high school he won a concerto contest and was a piano soloist in the youth symphony. His piano teacher convinced him that he should go to college at Michigan State. He went early, found his way around campus, and was ready when the fall semester began. At the suggestion of his teacher, he studied music therapy—using music as a means of therapy for people with disabilities.

Studying music at Michigan State was a wonderful experience. He developed many friends with mutual interests, and his personality blossomed. In his second year, he began to date a beautiful, sighted young woman who also was studying piano. For him, there was only one problem: She was a deeply committed Christian and the daughter of a Baptist minister.

This was a problem for Ken because in high school he had rebelled against the restrictive nature of the Christian faith as he had observed it in the Dutch Calvinist church of his parents. Yet he was very interested in the young woman, so he went with her to church. He tells what happened in his own words:

> Hers was a "countrified" southern Baptist church right in the middle of Grand Rapids. Though I didn't enjoy the music in the church, I loved the warmth and acceptance of the pastor and the congregation. Little by little I began to experience the love of God anew. One evening I went to the altar, weeping, to renew my commitment to Christ. The truth of faith is in listening to the story all over again—that the Infinite God loves us and has redeemed us. It is a mystery, but more real than anything I know. My life has been wrapped around by love by the same God who created me. For me, Jesus is the face that was put on love so that I could understand it.

After their marriage, Ken and his wife, Jane, worked in music therapy in two psychiatric hospitals. During this period he returned to Michigan State for a master's degree in music, and she enrolled in seminary. In 1972, Ken sang at a Billy Graham crusade in Cleveland, Ohio. After that crusade, requests "came in like crazy," as Ken put it. Since then he has been a freelance artist, composing music and performing in 170 concerts annually in churches, schools, colleges, and conferences. A highlight of his career to date was performing in the TV special "Crack in the Wall," produced to encourage persons with disabilities.

When I asked Ken if he had ever felt sorry for himself, he replied: "When I was growing up, sometimes I did; but I soon realized that blindness is a characteristic. Whether it becomes a handicap is up to the individual. I choose to accept my characteristic, laugh at my mistakes, surround myself with loving support, and trust God for the future."

What a philosophy! When I am tempted to feel sorry for myself because of difficulties, disappointments, or real or imagined wrongs, I hope I always will remember the evidence of God's love and grace that comes through a man like Ken Medema.

Steps to Moving Out of Self-Pity

1. All of us are tempted to feel sorry for ourselves because of life's difficulties and pains. Resist the temptation!
2. Never allow yourself to indulge in self-pity for more than fifteen minutes at a time. Otherwise, you will be held in its clutches. It becomes a downward spiral, going from self-pity to discouragement to despair to depression.

---

3. Don't play the "blame game." Take responsibility for your life and actions.

4. Remind yourself that self-pity destroys creativity.

5. Remember that self-pity begins with thoughts, and you can deliberately choose to change your thoughts. Heed the apostle Paul's advice to think on the things that are true, honorable, just, pure, pleasing, and commendable (see Philippians 4:8).

6. Stop and give thanks for your blessings. Remember Ken Medema's remarkable achievements despite a lifetime of physical blindness. He says it so well: "Blindness is only a characteristic. Whether it becomes a handicap is up to the individual."

7. Recall and say aloud the following biblical affirmations:

• "I can do all things through [Christ] who strengthens me" (Philippians 4:13).

• "I know the one in whom I have put my trust, and I am sure that he is able to guard until that day what I have entrusted to him" (2 Timothy 1:12).

• "With God all things are possible" (Matthew 19:26 NIV).

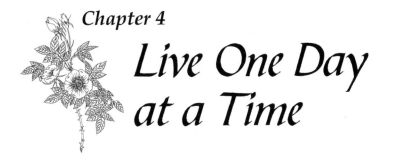

Chapter 4

Live One Day at a Time

So do not worry about tomorrow, for tomorrow will bring worries of its own.

—*Matthew 6:34*

It was a bitterly cold day during the height of the Christmas rush. Shopping seemed to have reached a fever pitch. There were crowds lined up at the counters, and people were crawling all over one another like ants in an anthill. I was weary of the whole scene, when suddenly an incident occurred that gave me fresh insight into life and a clearer perspective of what was going on around me.

The battle-fatigued saleslady spoke in a wooden voice as she handed a package to a young lady just ahead of me: "Merry Christmas, and happy New Year." The young customer replied in a clear, convincing tone: "It's going to be a happy year."

"But how do you know that?" asked the startled saleslady. "Because the year is made up of days, and if we live one day at a time and seek to make it happy, then we will have a happy year." With that, the cheery young lady flashed a contagious smile and hurried off down the aisle.

My weariness suddenly left me. I felt light and happy

all over. "She's right, you know," I said to the saleslady, whose tense face had relaxed into a broad smile. "I know," she replied, "and I hope I can remember it for the next two weeks."

As I continued my shopping, I thought of how important the principle of living one day at a time is to our happiness. As a result, I sat down and wrote a list of resolutions that I could use each day. I entitled the list "Just for Today."

JUST FOR TODAY, I will have a quiet half hour in which I read the scriptures and other inspirational books, pray, and seek God's direction and perspective on my life.

JUST FOR TODAY, I will resist the temptation to live in the past or worry about the future. I will focus on, enjoy, and learn from today. I will remember the words of the psalmist: "This is the day that the LORD has made; let us rejoice and be glad in it" (Psalm 118:24).

JUST FOR TODAY, I won't try to solve all my problems at once. I can do something I don't like for twenty-four hours if I remember that I don't have to keep it up for a lifetime. In retrospect, I realize that if I had known the number of dishes I would wash, or diapers I would change, or meals I would cook in a lifetime of marriage, I probably would have married Ralph Mohney anyway; but I wouldn't have been so enthusiastic about it. To quote Dr. Robert Schuller: "Life by the yard is hard; but life by the inch is a cinch."

JUST FOR TODAY, I will take nothing for granted. I will be grateful for people who love me and whom I can love—family and friends. I will do someone a good turn and try not to get "found out." I will do at least two things I don't want to do—just for exercise.

JUST FOR TODAY, I will not be a mental loafer. I will read something that requires effort, thought, and concentration. I will not allow my mind to be bogged down in critical, resentful, or evil thoughts. The apostle Paul's words to the Philippians will be a reminder to think purely and positively. In Philippians 4:8 he suggests that we think on the things that are true, honest, just, pure, lovely, and of good report.

JUST FOR TODAY, I will remember that my future good health depends primarily on my ability to stay fit physically. I will eat nutritious food, exercise for at least twenty minutes a day, walk in the out-of-doors when possible, and get enough rest.

JUST FOR TODAY, I will laugh often. It will be good for my "internal jogging." I will laugh at myself because it will keep me from perfectionism and will remind me that I am not in charge of the universe. In addition, I will be more relaxed and more fun to be around.

JUST FOR TODAY, I will choose to be happy. It was Abraham Lincoln who said: "Most folks are about as happy as they make up their minds to be." In her delightful book *Splashes of Joy in the Cesspools of Life*, Barbara Johnson writes: "Pain is inevitable, but misery is a choice." I believe that happiness also is a choice.

JUST FOR TODAY, I will enjoy the beauty of God's creation and express my gratitude through service to others. I want to remember that this day—and this century—is a gift from God. What I do with this day is my gift to God.

I challenge you to make such a list! It will lift your spirit as you discover what this year will bring.

We can learn from the adage: "Yesterday is history; tomorrow is a mystery. Today is a gift. That's why we call it 'the present.'"

Steps to Living One Day at a Time

1. Remember that each day is a gift from God. What you do with it is your gift to God.
2. Spend thirty minutes each day reading God's Word and other inspirational materials, praying, and seeking God's guidance.
3. Resist the temptation to live in the past and worry about tomorrow. Live in "day-tight compartments."
4. Don't try to solve all your problems at once. Remember Dr. Robert Schuller's wise words: "Life by the yard is hard; life by the inch is a cinch."
5. Don't take anything for granted. See life as an incredible gift—not as an entitlement.
6. Read something daily that requires effort, thought, and concentration.
7. Don't get bogged down in critical, negative, or evil thoughts.
8. Work on physical fitness daily: eat nutritious food, exercise, and relax.
9. Choose to be happy.
10. Recall and say aloud these biblical affirmations:
   • "Do not worry about tomorrow..." (Matthew 6:34).
   • "This is the day that the LORD has made; let us rejoice and be glad in it" (Psalm 118:24).

Chapter 5

Appreciate Sight and Develop Insight

I am fearfully and wonderfully made.

—Psalm 139:14

My mother had eyes in the back of her head! I'm sure of it! When she was in one room and we children were in another, she knew exactly what we were doing. Even if we were playing in the yard and she was in the house, she seemed to be able to see us when we were getting into trouble. It was years later before I understood that there are different kinds of sight—that we "see" in many ways.

Physical sight, obviously, is a most precious gift, which we should never take for granted. As a junior in high school, I went on our school's annual spring trip to Washington, D.C. Surely there is no more beautiful place in the world than our nation's capital in the springtime. The Japanese cherry trees were in bloom, and it was like awakening every morning to a fairyland of soft color and fragrance. On our second day of sightseeing, we went to the Lincoln Memorial. Seated on one of the steps was a blind man. He was wearing a sign that read: "It's springtime and I'm blind." Since that day, every time I am aware of beauty in the physical world, I give special thanks to God for the gift of physical sight.

The eye is more intricately complex than the most sophisticated camera. A report from the Department of Ophthalmology at Harvard University says that there are millions of electrical connections in the eye that handle over one and a half million messages simultaneously. If we were to exercise the muscles in our legs as we do the muscles in our eyes, we would have to walk fifty miles every day. Think of what happens. We receive an image through the lens of our eyes. The image is focused on the retina, where millions of receptors flash it to the brain at a speed of three hundred miles an hour. We see the image in intricate detail and living color. Truly miraculous! In the words of the psalmist, each of us is "fearfully and wonderfully made" (Psalm 139:14).

In addition to physical sight, we have mental sight. Do you recall a mathematical equation that made no sense at all to you? Then someone explained it to you, and you said, "I see." As a child, math was my least favorite subject. For one thing, I disliked having to sit still and learn multiplication tables when there were so many more interesting things to do. I can still "see" my father patiently calling out multiplication tables and explaining math problems to me—that is, until I got to algebra and geometry—and mathematics suddenly made sense to me. It was a mental "aha!" experience.

Physical and mental sight are both marvelous, but an even greater gift is the ability to see with our hearts. In the Bible, the word *heart* includes intellect, emotion, and will. The eyes of our hearts, therefore, include comprehension, discernment, insight, wisdom, vision, and perception. Our "heart eyes" are given to us so that we may see what God sees.

In his book *Lonely Husbands, Lonely Wives,* Dennis

Rainey suggests that two persons can be married to each other, go lots of places together, and still feel lonely in their inner worlds. Likewise, in his book *Congratulations: God Believes in You*, Dr. Lloyd Ogilvie tells of a woman who said to him: "How I wish my husband could see the real me. He looks right past me. He has a preconceived set of theories and everybody has to fit into them." As I read those words, I thought how universal that cry really is—and not just from wives. This cry also may be heard from husbands to wives, children to parents, friends to friends, employees to employers, and even parents to children.

Just as we can develop cataracts on our physical eyes—causing our sight to grow dimmer and dimmer until, finally, we require surgery—so, too, we can develop cataracts of our soul and lose our spiritual sight when we are separated from our source: God. We need to have our spiritual cataracts removed so that the cloudy, murky, fuzzy veil falls away and we can see people and circumstances as God would have us see them.

Perhaps the greatest gift of sight is the ability to envision. The late William James said that most of us use only one-tenth of our potential. But the good news is that God has given us the ability to project ourselves into the future—to stand outside ourselves and see not only who we are but also who we can become.

All of the material things we see—houses, churches, schools, hospitals, cars, clothing, and so forth—were first envisioned by someone before those things became realities. This is the kind of vision that led a small boy named Abraham Lincoln from a log cabin in Illinois to the presidency of a great nation. Imagine what can happen if we envision what God envisions for us—and for our homes, our schools, our churches, and our world—and then set out to make those dreams become realities.

We all have the capacity for envisioning. Remember, if we don't use it, we lose it. Perhaps each of us should ask the question: "How much of the gift of sight am I using?"

Steps for Appreciating and Improving the Gifts of Sight and Insight

1. Reflect often on the psalmist's declaration: "I am fearfully and wonderfully made" (Psalm 139:14). Allow its meaning to become more and more significant.

2. Treasure your eyesight. Remember that if we were to exercise the muscles in our legs as we do the muscles in our eyes, we would have to walk fifty miles a day!

3. Each day as you see some of the beauty of God's creation, take time to say "thank you" for the gift of your *physical sight*.

4. Each time you learn something new—which should be every day—stop to express gratitude for the gift of *mental* sight.

5. Seek to develop your emotional sight, which is the ability to have sensitivity toward and care for another person. This gift is especially important to family life.

6. Understand that the gift of insight is the ability to see beyond "what is" to "what can be." Use this gift to see your home, church, community, and world as God sees them. You may develop this gift by staying close to God through regular Bible reading, prayer, and worship. As you follow God's example, you will be empowered by the Holy Spirit to see clearly—in every sense of the word.

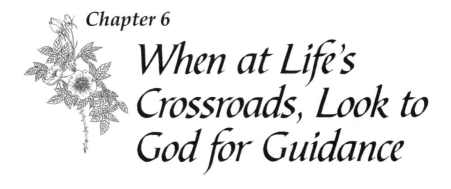

Chapter 6

When at Life's Crossroads, Look to God for Guidance

Trust in the LORD with all your heart, and do not rely on your own insight. In all your ways acknowledge him, and he will make straight your paths.

—Proverbs 3:5-6

*H*ave you ever taken the wrong road or become confused about the directions you were given? Have you ever been lost?

How well I remember taking the wrong road with a good friend when we were both seniors in college. Margaret and I were driving to her home for spring holidays. It wasn't as if we were taking a new route. She drove regularly from Greensboro to her home in Asheville, North Carolina, where she had lived since she was five years old. Yet we ended up taking the wrong road. For one thing, we started late, just before dusk; but our main problem was that we both liked to talk, and we had lots to talk about. We were busily discussing a recent campus incident, as well as firming up plans for our holiday week. Suddenly, Margaret realized she didn't see any familiar landmarks. Then we discovered that we had gone fifty miles in the wrong direction.

Many of us do the same thing when we come to life's crossroads. How often we forget that the great God of the universe is not only willing but also eager to point the way and lead us back to the right road when we have taken a wrong turn. Scriptures in both the Old and New Testaments assure us that God *will* guide us if only we will give God the chance.

There are some who do not believe in God's guidance. They believe that we are "biological accidents" who must live by our instincts and wits. Others have a less negative view, believing that God created the world. They even attend church from time to time. But the notion that God gives them directions for their personal living is far too remote for them to grasp. Perhaps this is because they don't want God intruding in their lives.

I worked with a middle-aged woman many years ago who had that kind of attitude. Miss Maude, as we called her, never married. In fact, our employer thought she would be with him for life. Then a widower temporarily moved into town. He gave Miss Maude a big "rush," and one Monday morning she announced they were to be married in two weeks and were to move to Boston.

Our employer must have had visions of chaos running through his mind as he thought of the office without this competent woman. Being a religious man, he said, "Miss Maude, this is very sudden. Don't you think we ought to pray about this?" Quick as a flash she replied, "Don't you dare!" This was the closest she had ever come to getting a husband, and she wasn't about to let anyone—not even God—mess up her plans! Several months later, Miss Maude returned to our office. She was much wiser but, unfortunately, one hundred thousand dollars poorer than when she had left.

Many of us are equally shortsighted at times, and it is only in retrospect that we realize we have taken the wrong road. May we remember that God is ready and waiting to give us the guidance we need. All we have to do is ask!

Steps to Take at Life's Crossroads

1. Remember that God places "signposts" all along life's journey. You can find these signposts in both the Old and New Testaments. You can also discern them through prayer, silence, and guidance from a Christian pastor, friend, or counselor.

2. Trust God's direction. You can count on God's promises!

3. When you do not seek God's guidance but go headlong on your way only to crash, remember that you can go back for direction. God will not save you from the consequences of your actions, but God *will* give you another opportunity. We serve a God of second chances.

4. Always be willing to help others who have taken the wrong road. Don't tell them what to do or how to do it, unless they ask. Instead, listen and be ready to point the way to the One who can set their feet on the right path.

5. Wherever you find yourself on life's journey, be a representative of Christ by showing his love to others.

6. Recall and say aloud these biblical affirmations:

• "The one who began a good work among you will bring it to completion . . ." (Philippians 1: 6).

• "In all these things we are more than conquerors through him who loved us" (Romans 8:37).

• "If God is for [me], who can be against [me]?" (Romans 8:31 NIV).

• "I will never leave you or forsake you" (Hebrews 13:5).

• "I am with you always, to the end of the age" (Matthew 28:20).

Chapter 7

Develop Your Charisma

Stephen, full of grace and power, did great wonders and signs among the people. . . . But they could not withstand the wisdom and the Spirit with which he spoke.

—Acts 6:8, 10

Y ou've got charisma!" These were my thoughts as I listened and watched Dr. William Morrison speak at a seminar at which I was a participant. There was an almost indefinable personal magnetism about him—a radiance, a sparkle. His eyes shone and his smile was a passport to immediate trust and confidence.

His appeal was far more than the ability to communicate his obvious knowledge and expertise in the subject under discussion: successful life management. It was more than his self-confidence, evidenced by a calm, cool composure and an ability to take charge. It was even more than his impeccable grooming, his thorough preparation, his strong moral character, and his sense of humor—though these were all impressive.

"What is this thing called charisma?" I asked myself as I returned to my hotel room. *Webster's Ninth New Collegiate Dictionary* defines charisma as "a personal magic of leadership arousing popular loyalty or enthusiasm for a public figure." Dr. William Campbell, a Christian psychiatrist, may not be a public figure per se, but he certainly had enthusiastic support from his seminar participants.

Today there is much confusion about the word *charisma*. Everybody talks about it; we all want it; we expect it of our leaders; but few of us truly know what it is. The first time I heard the word *charisma*, it was used to describe the late President John F. Kennedy and his leadership style. I later learned that the word was introduced into popular usage by a scholar writing in *Forbes* magazine in the early seventies. The author placed it under a picture of John L. Lewis to describe the labor leader's influence with unions. *Time* magazine then picked up the word and made it the intellectual word of the week.

It was in 1975—when the word *charisma* was being used in advertising to describe everything from underwear to boots—that I began a serious study of the word. I discovered that what we call charisma in certain people is little more than personality strength. The real meaning of the word, originated by the Greeks, is "to show favor" or "grace gifted." It was used in Greek mythology to identify three graces as gifts or favors from the gods.

The apostle Paul adopted the word charisma and used it to describe the lifestyle of persons who had authentically received the grace of God through Christ. This is the message of "amazing grace" found in the book of Romans. Paul wrote, "We have gifts that differ according to the grace given to us" (12:6).

Paul was saying, in effect, that personal magnetism comes not from developing certain personality traits, but from the overwhelming knowledge that we are loved—which causes us to exude a kind of confidence and "chosen-ness" that is appealing. Our magnetism is so much more evident, then, when we have accepted the grace of God through Christ.

This explains the appeal of my seminar leader, Dr. Morrison. Obviously he has worked to develop his God-given talents of communication. He has used self-discipline to study and be thoroughly prepared. He has learned the importance of being proactive. He also has developed a sense of humor and has given special attention to grooming. But his dynamic power of influence is rooted in something far greater than these.

Though it was a secular setting, Dr. Morrison openly shared his personal experience of Christ with the large seminar audience. He told us that he wasn't very successful in managing his life until he invited Christ to be Lord of his life. He explained that though he always had been a nominal Christian and a somewhat regular church attendant, he had remained in control of all his decisions. In fact, he admitted that he had carefully orchestrated his life around clearly defined but completely self-centered goals. He even had tried to orchestrate the lives of his family members. It wasn't until everything began to unravel and he began to have a sense of terrible emptiness that he sought, through the help of a minister, a personal relationship with Christ. Only then, he said, did he become integrated at the center of his being. Only then did he discover who he is and whose he is. His suggestion to our group was that our lives need to be grounded in something bigger than we are.

Dr. Morrison's calm confidence comes from the assurance that he is loved, forgiven, and empowered. Connected to the ultimate Power Force, he allows the Holy Spirit of God to empower his natural talents and "gift" him with amazing grace. That's real charisma. Are you seeking it?

Steps to Developing Charisma

1. Remember that the apostle Paul adopted the word *charisma* from the Greeks. He used it to describe those who were grace-gifted by Christ.

2. Stay close to Christ, who is the instrument through whom God's grace is mediated to us.

3. Remember that you don't earn God's grace by doing good works; you do good works because you have opened yourself to receive God's grace. It is a gift!

4. Daily welcome Christ's presence in your life and seek to be more like him. As you do this, others will see in you the fruit of the Spirit. According to Galatians 5:22-23, this fruit includes love, joy, peace, patience, gentleness, goodness, faith, humility, and self-control. When others see these attributes, they call it charisma.

5. Believe that you are "grace gifted." According to the apostle Paul, as Christ lives in our lives through the Holy Spirit, we also are given specific spiritual gifts. Among these are leadership, teaching, administration, wisdom, knowledge, hospitality, and giving. (See Romans 12, 1 Corinthians 12, and Ephesians 4.)

6. When you add to your spiritual gifts a deep love of people, a commitment to excellence, and a willingness to serve Christ, you truly will become a charismatic personality.

Chapter 8

Cope with Fatigue

Those who wait for the LORD shall renew their strength, they shall mount up with wings like eagles, they shall run and not be weary, they shall walk and not faint.

—*Isaiah 40:31*

W hat's your problem?" I overheard the exasperated mother ask her teenage son, who obviously was having an attitude problem that day in the airport. It was apparent that the grumpy boy was complaining and making his mother's trip miserable. Evidently, a part of his problem was that he didn't want to go wherever it was they were going.

That same question could be asked of most of us on a more serious level. Even if we are not dealing with crises, most of us are dealing with some ordinary problems that can wear us down and keep us from effective, meaningful living. And if we do not cope well with those problems, they can make our lives miserable.

Fatigue is a widespread and chronic problem for people of varying ages. In a recent seven-day period, I counted twenty-two times when I heard someone say, "I'm tired," "I've had it," "I can't go on like this," or some similar expression of fatigue, weariness, stress, or boredom. And those commenting were not just older people. They ranged in age from ten to eighty-two!

How do we cope with the "blahs"? How, indeed, do we learn to energize ourselves? Let me share some suggested solutions I have learned through observation and experience.

An obvious first step is to be sure that our fatigue is not the result of illness. Fatigue is an early symptom of many serious conditions and diseases. So we need to have regular physical checkups.

Second, we need to get plenty of rest and give up the common pastime of "burning the candle at both ends." If we are to be energized for daily living, we must learn to balance our work with relaxation, recreation, and worship.

Third, we need to exercise regularly. As strange as it may sound, exercise actually counteracts fatigue. The last thing I want to do when I am feeling weary is to exercise. Yet a brisk walk, a two-mile bike ride, or thirty minutes in the pool can make me feel like a new person. It energizes my body and clarifies my thinking. So, when you feel weary in your body and mind, get those muscles moving. Don't be a couch potato!

Fourth, we must remember that tired thoughts result in tired bodies. Negative, unhappy, gloomy thoughts cause muscles to sag and vitality to disappear mysteriously. I remember calling on a woman in a nursing home. She looked exhausted and weak. Yet when I told her that her sister had telephoned and would be coming to see her the following day, it was as if a sudden surge of strength went through every cell of her body. Her posture improved. Her eyes lit up. Even her voice became stronger. The only thing that had changed was her thinking. Anticipation replaced lethargy. When the apostle Paul tells us in Philippians 4:8 to think about things that are true, honest, just, pure, lovely, and of good report, he is giving us a formula for vitality.

Fifth, each of us needs a purpose, a mission, a dream. Having something to anticipate and work toward generates energy and enthusiasm. It can be a big dream or only a small activity. As a child, do you remember how excited you were the night before you went on vacation? You could hardly sleep and awakened early to bounce out of bed. That's the kind of eager enthusiasm that comes from anticipating a desired activity, event, or accomplishment.

Several years ago I was fascinated by a family who seemed to have continuous enthusiasm and vitality. They weren't bogged down in the ho-hum existence so characteristic of many families. Their four children ranged in age from four to fourteen. Both parents worked. They had enough pressures to make everybody tired. What, then, was the secret of their energy? When I inquired, the father told me this: "In addition to being people of faith and love, we always have something for the family to anticipate. We [including the children] plan some outing or excursion for the family every two weeks. These include such things as picnics, overnight camping, biking, swimming, water skiing, movies, or putt-putt golf. As a result, we are usually talking enthusiastically about what we did or what we are going to do. Anticipation helps to avoid the rut of ho-hum living."

Sixth, we need to get organized. Being disorganized can overwhelm us and keep us tired. On the other hand, when we feel in control and on top of the situation, we feel strong and full of energy. So throw away the excess baggage from your life. Set goals, organize your efforts, and follow through. Don't procrastinate. Dreading to do something takes more energy than doing it. Find the help you need and say "no" to the trivialities. You soon will be on top of things.

Seventh, we should stay close to energetic people. When we are with complaining, self-pitying, negative people, we find that the energy is drained out of us. Once when I was a patient in the hospital, a negative worrier came to visit me. Though I appreciated her effort in driving across town to see me, it took me hours to regain my strength after her energy-depleting conversation. In contrast, positive, enthusiastic, faith-filled people motivated and energized me. It is the same for all of us.

Eighth, and finally, we must keep our faith alive. Each of us needs time to regenerate our energy supply through regular Bible reading, prayer, meditation, and corporate worship. As Isaiah 30:15 reminds us: "In quietness and in trust shall be your strength."

In the book *Aging and God*, researchers from Duke University Medical Center report that faith not only re-energizes us but also helps us to live longer and better lives. Through studies they have discovered that people of faith who attend church frequently have lower blood pressure and fewer strokes; lower rates of depression, anxiety, and alcoholism; and a greater sense of well-being. What's more, people of faith adapt better to the rigors of physical illness and disability.

In a sermon he preached in 1972, Dr. Norman Vincent Peale said that General Douglas MacArthur believed that faith brings us not only strength and energy, but also youthful spirits. Then he shared this excerpt from a speech General MacArthur made to a Los Angeles audience in 1956:

> You are as young as your faith, as old as your doubts; as young as your confidence, as old as your fears; as young as your hopes, as old as your despair. In the central place of every heart there is the recording chamber. So long as it receives messages of beauty, hope, cheer and courage, so long are we young. When the wires are all

down and your heart is covered with the snows of pessimism and cynicism, then and only then are you growing old.

So, what's your problem? If it is fatigue, you can learn to energize yourself!

Steps to Coping with Fatigue

1. Have a physical checkup. Fatigue is often an early symptom of serious illness.
2. Don't "burn the candle at both ends." Your work needs to be balanced with relaxation, recreation, and worship.
3. Exercise regularly. Physical exercise counteracts fatigue.
4. Remember that negative and gloomy thoughts cause vitality to disappear quickly. The apostle Paul gives us the solution in Philippians 4:8, where he tells us to think about things that are true, honest, just, pure, lovely, and commendable.
5. Have a purpose, a mission, a dream. Having something to anticipate and work toward creates energy and enthusiasm.
6. Get organized. Feeling out of control can overwhelm us and keep us tired.
7. Surround yourself with positive, faith-filled friends who will motivate and energize you.
8. Keep your faith alive through regular prayer, Bible reading, and corporate worship.

Chapter 9

Love Yourself

You were bought with a price; therefore glorify God in your body.

—1 Corinthians 6:20

*I*t had been a long, hot day. In addition to my usual household and office responsibilities, there had been a church picnic at a retreat center. Though all of us enjoyed the great food and fellowship, we returned home debilitated and disheveled from so much exertion in ninety-degree weather. There was not so much as a breeze to allay the oppressive atmosphere. I felt like a double-fried egg.

I was so glad to be home and take a cool bath. Just at that moment, the telephone rang, and a weak voice on the other end said, "Nell, I have taken an overdose and I . . ." Her voice trailed off. I didn't have to wonder who it was. Emily was a young woman in her early thirties who had failed at just about everything that was important to her—jobs, friendships, and most recently, a relationship with a man she had hoped to marry.

When I repeated her name and didn't get a response, I said very loudly: "I'll be there, Emily. Hold on." While I quickly slipped into some clothes, I called her next-door neighbor, who had a key to Emily's apartment. She told me that she and her husband would get Emily to the hospital and I could meet them there. Emily was almost gone by the time they reached the hospital. Even after her stomach had been pumped, it was "touch and go" for forty-eight hours.

On the day that it was certain Emily would recover—without brain damage—I talked quietly with her. I thanked her for calling me and told her how fortunate she was to be alive. Then I explained that her doctor had arranged appointments for her with a very competent counselor, who would help her discover the source of her despair. I shall never forget her looking directly at me and saying, "I know the source, Nell. Very simply, it's that I hate myself."

She was right on target. Early conditioning from well-intentioned but negative and overly strict parents had given her a self-image of unworthiness, stupidity, and inadequacy. This and her other negative experiences had so programmed her subconscious mind that she never expected to succeed in anything. As a result, whenever she was about to succeed in an endeavor, she would do something to sabotage it, so that once again she could conform to her negative self-image. Months of counseling and a dynamic spiritual experience turned Emily's life in a new direction.

Perhaps the greatest discovery in the field of mental health during the last forty years has been the importance of self-image—the desperate need each of us has to feel good about ourselves. We need to know that we are unique, that we are worthy, and that, with God's help, we are adequate to face life's pressures and problems.

A young lawyer once asked Jesus which was the greatest commandment, and Jesus replied: " 'You shall love the Lord your God with all your heart, and with all your soul, and with all your mind.' This is the greatest and first commandment. And a second is like it: 'You shall love your neighbor as yourself'" (Matthew 22:35-39). Jesus knew that we cannot adequately love another person unless we have received God's love and can love and respect ourselves.

Once I heard a Christian psychologist say that when we encounter a person who is constantly bitter, continually critical, always complaining, and repeatedly saying hurtful and cruel things to others, we can be sure we are dealing with someone who does not like himself or herself. This brooding bitterness is a projection of his or her own self-loathing.

Even when we have a good self-image, sometimes we simply have had a bad day and end up blaming those around us. I laugh when I remember the story a bishop told on himself. He had had a very bad day and felt that he had made some unwise decisions. When he reached home, he was unhappy and frustrated. On that particular day, his wife had bought him a new suit. When he saw it, nothing about the suit pleased him. He decided that it was the wrong style, the wrong color, and the wrong size. In exasperation, his wife said, "Okay, I'll take it back."

The next day was a great day for the bishop. Everything seemed to go harmoniously. He arrived home feeling good about himself and his life. When he went into his bedroom, he noticed a suit hanging on the closet door. Obviously, his wife must have exchanged the first suit for another one. When he tried it on, he was delighted. He modeled it for his wife and said, "Everything about this suit is just right. In fact, it's perfect. You did a great job." She smiled and replied, "I didn't exchange the suit. That's the same one you tried on yesterday." The difference was apparent. On the second day, the bishop felt good about himself.

If this can happen on a day when we don't feel good about ourselves, think what can happen when we really hate ourselves. I am so sorry for those who try to overcome their self-loathing through drugs, alcohol, compulsive buying, sexual promiscuity, compulsive gambling, or some other escape. These unhealthy habits can produce oversensitivity, jealousy, bitterness, negativism, guilt, self-pity, restlessness, and constant unhappiness.

If we are going to live creative, meaningful, and productive lives, then we must remember that we are created in the image of God, redeemed by Christ, and empowered by the Holy Spirit. As children of God, we are special and worthy of love—not because of what we have done, but because of what God has done for us through Jesus Christ. Let us claim our birthright!

Steps to Learning to Love Yourself

1. Recognize that early conditioning from abusive or even well-intentioned but negative and overly strict parents can give you a sense of unworthiness—or even cause you to hate yourself. As a result, your subconscious mind may cause you to sabotage any attempt at success.

2. If self-loathing is severe, you may need to see a Christian counselor. Otherwise, you may find yourself "escaping" through drugs, alcohol, compulsive buying, gambling, sexual promiscuity, or some other unhealthy habit.

3. Recall Jesus' teaching that tells us we cannot adequately love another person unless we have received God's love and can love and respect ourselves (see Matthew 22:35-39).

4. Remember that you are special and worthy of love—not because of what you have done, but because of what God has done for you through Jesus Christ (see John 3:16 and 1 Corinthians 6:20).
5. Never forget that you are created in the image of God, redeemed by Jesus Christ, and empowered by the Holy Spirit. That is a powerful heritage!

Chapter 10

Guard Against Negativism

Keep your heart with all vigilance, for from it flow the springs of life.

—*Proverbs 4:23*

Recently I read this statement in a health magazine: "More people are depressed in January than any other month of the year." Instantly my mind responded with, "Amen—especially when it rains so much." Just as quickly I began to think of many things other than the weather that can cause the January blahs.

Many people experience an emotional letdown after the excitement and festivities of the holidays. For some, this letdown results from overspending, overeating, or other excesses. For others, their expectations for Christmas were too high, and disappointment hangs over them like an ominous cloud. Then there are those who are hurting emotionally, and the festivities of the holidays seem to wash against the stone wall of their pain. Perhaps they are suffering from separation from relatives, the death of a loved one, a recent divorce, worry about making a living in a very competitive society, or the fear of global terrorism. The truth is, we can have the January blahs any time of the year. Many of us are experiencing a down day *right now*.

What do you do when you find yourself sinking into negativism, despair, or even depression? In my own experience, I have learned to stand guard over my thoughts. We must realize that feelings come from our thoughts—not from our circumstances—and we control our thoughts. For example, if you are driving down the highway and see a car headed straight for you in your lane, you push your internal panic button. The act of seeing the car could be labeled "A," and the panic you feel could be labeled "C." The "B" is in between the two; it is your thought: "That car is going to hit me. I could be killed." The thought triggers the feeling. So, if we think gloomy, negative, depressed *thoughts,* we are going to have gloomy, negative, depressed *feelings.*

Long ago Marcus Aurelius, the Roman ruler, wrote: "Our lives are dyed the color of our thoughts." Even longer ago than that, the author of the book of Proverbs wrote: "As he thinketh in his heart, so is he" (Proverbs 23:7 KJV). None of us is able to choose the time in which we live, and many of the externals of life are beyond our control. Yet all of us can control our thinking and choose the things that occupy our minds. As we do so, we create not only our feelings but also the world in which we live.

The second way to beat negativism is to start each day well. For me, that means conditioning my mind with gratitude—counting my blessings—before I get out of bed. Then comes exercise, my quiet time, and a good breakfast.

Have you ever awakened feeling sluggish and not wanting to get out of bed, only to find that after five minutes of exercise, you are beginning to look forward to the day? I once attended a seminar in which the leader asked us to jump up and down as if we had received the most wonderful news; and while we were jumping, we were to say, "I am so depressed. I feel terrible." We discovered that it was almost impossible to do both. When we keep our muscles moving and our circulation going, it is hard to be depressed—or even to pretend it!

The most important segment of my early-morning routine is my thirty-minute quiet time. After exercise, a bath, and a cup of coffee, I go to my designated spot: a comfortable chair near a window overlooking a small lake. There I relax my body and fill my mind with spiritual nutrients from the Bible and other inspirational materials. Then I think about what I've read and how it applies to my life. In my prayers, I save time for quietness to receive God's guidance, which are the creative ideas that come from God—and which, I believe, God wants to give each of us.

Having nourished my mind and spirit, I eat a nutritious breakfast to energize my body. When I don't eat balanced meals, my body sags as well as my spirit. Once I heard former Congressman Ed Forman say that a sure way to stay in a bad mood all day is to get up late, skip breakfast, and tear off to work at breakneck speed.

A third way to overcome negativism is to include laughter in each day. I didn't understand how laughter affects our bodies until I read an article written by Dr. William Fry, Jr., of Stanford Medical School. He said that laughter is a form of physical exertion. It accelerates the heart rate, raises blood pressure, speeds up breathing, increases oxygen consumption, gives muscles of the face and stomach a workout, and relaxes muscles not involved in laughing. In short, laughter gives our entire system an invigorating lift.

Persons who have visited Dr. Albert Schweitzer's famous hospital at Lambaréné say that he employed humor as a way of reducing tension often caused by the hot temperature and humidity. It is reported that laughter was probably the most important course at dinner at that hospital, and that it was amazing to see staff members rejuvenated by Dr. Schweitzer's wry humor.

Once while speaking to a group on the importance of humor, I recommended the book *The Humor of Christ* by Elton Trueblood. Later my hostess for the evening sent me a copy of a painting of Jesus laughing. It was a wonderful gift, and I keep it on my desk as a reminder to keep life in perspective.

Another good remedy for negativism and depression is music. We read of people through the centuries having their spirits lifted by music. The Old Testament tells of a depressed King Saul calling for young David to play his harp so that Saul's spirit could be soothed. I think I know how King Saul must have felt at those times, for there are many wonderful hymns that lift my spirit instantly when I hear or sing them. In fact, I've often wondered if congregational singing is included in most services of worship for the purpose of lifting the spirits of the worshipers.

Finally, with God's help, we can *choose* to be happy rather than depressed. Remember, we are not born happy. Happiness comes as we give ourselves to great and worthy causes; as we give ourselves in loving actions to other people; and as we give ourselves confidently to a God who can keep us hopeful about the future.

 ## Steps to Overcoming Negativism

1. Remember that feelings come from thoughts, so guard your thoughts.

---

2. Start each day with gratitude, a quiet devotional time, exercise, and a nutritious breakfast.

3. Remember the importance of laughter. It will give your entire system an invigorating lift.

4. Use music to overcome negativism.

5. With God's help, *choose* daily to be happy, not miserable.

6. Stay close to Christ, who can keep you hopeful about the future.

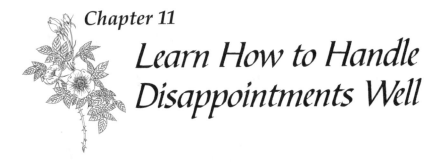

Chapter 11

Learn How to Handle Disappointments Well

My father David could not build a house for the name of the LORD his God because of the warfare with which his enemies surrounded him. . . . So I [Solomon] intend to build a house for the name of the LORD my God.

—*1 Kings 5:3, 5*

*H*er voice quivered as she told me the news: "I didn't get the promotion. They brought in a young man from outside the company."

My response was immediate: "But your supervisor had promised that job to you, and you have given long hours of overtime work. You've also given up most of your social life in preparation for the new position."

"I know," she replied glumly. "It just doesn't seem fair."

The same week I received that call from a thirty-eight-year-old woman, a middle-age man told me how, as a young man, he had been devastated when his fiancée had broken their engagement after the invitations had been mailed.

Disappointments are a universal experience. They start when we are children and continue as long as we live. Our ability or inability to handle them skillfully can make the difference between our happiness and unhappiness.

Some of our disappointments, though they may seem

large at the time, actually are small and inconsequential. These disappointments become easier to handle as we mature—things such as having to postpone a picnic because of a torrential rain, missing a vacation trip because of sickness, learning that a friend has failed us, and so forth. Other disappointments are more catastrophic. Yet whether major or minor, *all* of life's disappointments can be handled successfully. What is the formula? I believe the answer is fourfold: *feel, evaluate, pray,* and then *act*.

First, face your disappointments and allow yourself to feel disappointment, anger, or loss—rather than denying these feelings by keeping them out of your conscious mind. The woman who didn't get the promotion said this to me: "I allowed myself to feel upset, disappointed, angry, and full of self-pity for twenty-four hours. Then I took time to evaluate where I could make my best contribution. Only then was I ready to move on with my life." In other words, she allowed herself to feel the disappointment for a brief time without letting it degenerate into discouragement and depression.

Second, evaluate. Try to be objective enough to determine how much of your reaction is due to a bruised ego and how much represents real betrayal or lack of trust. Then objectively determine your next step. In the case of the missed promotion, the woman had to determine whether or not to leave the company. When her anger subsided, she realized that her supervisor had not actually promised her the position. He had indicated that she would be among those considered for it. She also realized that she still had opportunity for professional growth in that company, and that most of her friends were there. So she stayed and worked cooperatively with the man chosen for the position. In less than a year, she received an even better promotion. If she had been uncooperative or otherwise had exhibited a bad attitude, that never would have happened.

Third, pray for guidance. Disappointments really can become God's appointments. In the case of the broken engagement, the man had already seen red flags signaling trouble with his fiancée, but he hadn't really wanted to pay attention. Only later, when he was happily married to another person, could he fully see that his big disappointment actually had been God's appointment.

Fourth, and finally, act. Don't bog down in self-pity or inertia, but move on with your life. In the Bible we read how King David yearned to build the Temple in Jerusalem. That privilege, however, went to his son, Solomon. King David faced a great disappointment, yet he chose to provide Solomon with all the materials needed to complete the job.

Thomas Carlyle, one of the greatest writers of all time, told of a disappointment that could have destroyed his entire career. He set out to write a very serious book. It took him four years of hard work because he wrote the book in his own hand. Finally, he completed the last page. Joyously he took the finished manuscript to his friend, John Stuart Mill, and asked him to read it. It took Mr. Mill several days to read that wonderful manuscript. As he read it, he realized that it was truly a great literary achievement. Late one night as he finished the last page, he left the manuscript pages by his chair in the den of his home. The next morning when the maid came, she saw the papers on the floor and thought they had been discarded. So she threw them into the fire, and they were burned. When Mr. Mill realized what had happened, he felt great agony of mind as he went across the field to his friend's home and told him that his work of long years had been destroyed. Carlyle replied, "It's all right. I'm sure I can start over in the morning and do it again."

Finally, after great apologies, John Mill left and started back to his home. As Carlyle watched his friend walking through the field, he said to his wife, "Poor Mill. I feel so sorry for him. I did not want him to see how crushed I really am." Then, heaving a sigh, he said, "Well the manuscript is gone, so I had better start writing again."

It was a long, hard process, but Thomas Carlyle finally completed the work. He walked away from his disappointment. He could do nothing about a manuscript that was burned. Likewise, there are times in our own lives when we can do nothing to change a situation. We simply must move on with our lives.

When floods came to our area, I realized that despite the devastation, there is always a rich deposit of topsoil following a flood. This can be seen most easily in the Mississippi delta. So it is in our lives. The floods of disappointment, frustration, and sorrow come sweeping over us, but we keep on going; and somehow, out of the disappointments, we find ourselves enriched. After the flood, the beauty of life can become even more beautiful.

Steps to Overcoming Disappointment

1. Whether they are major or minor, face your disappointments and allow yourself to feel disappointment, anger, or loss. But be sure to limit the time for doing this so that you do not become discouraged or depressed. Usually twenty-four hours is a good time span.

2. Evaluate. Take time to be objective enough to decide whether your disappointment comes from a bruised ego, a betrayal, or a real tragedy. Only then can you determine your next step.

3. Pray for guidance. Remember there are times when our disappointments are God's appointments.

4. Then act. Don't bog down in self-pity or inertia; instead, move on with your life.

Chapter 12

Go Through Midlife Without a Crisis

When I was a child, I spoke like a child, I thought like a child, I reasoned like a child; when I became an adult, I put an end to childish ways.

—*1 Corinthians 13:11*

I've heard everything! For years I've heard people blame problems such as drinking excessively or having extramarital affairs or even being accident prone on a midlife crisis. I once read that a woman in the West had blamed her cruelty to animals on a midlife crisis. Can you believe that?

Is there really such a thing as a midlife crisis? Is it a myth or a reality? I believe that whether we call it a *crisis* or a *transition* depends upon what we consider important in life—our value system and purpose for living—and how well we have dealt with our past, including whether we have forgiven ourselves, our parents, and others who have hurt us.

There is no doubt that middle age is a definable stage in life through which we all pass. It has been called "middlescence" by some because the changes in body and mind are as intense as those in adolescence. Like some teenagers who seem to breeze through adolescence, there are some adults who go through middle age with relative smoothness and emerge as more mature, more creative, and more authentic people. On the other hand, some people deny the entire experience, which leads to a withering of the self; and still others basically self-destruct. So, let's look at this period of life honestly. What is middle age? If you are thirty, you say it starts at forty; if you are forty, you say it begins at fifty; if you are fifty, you say sixty. Most social scientists say middle age is the period from age thirty-five to sixty-five—or even older, now that we are living longer.

Several years ago as I prepared an address on "The Christian Approach to the Stages of Life," I found many materials on the topic of midlife. In one resource, the description of this period of life was written anonymously and with a "tongue-in-cheek" attitude. A part of the description included these words:

> Middle age is when you are too young to get on Social Security and too old to get another job; when you are warned to slow down by a doctor instead of a policeman; when you want to see how long your car will last instead of how fast it will go; when the telephone rings on Saturday night and you hope it isn't for you; when you stop criticizing the older generation and start criticizing the younger generation; when you believe that in a week or two you'll feel as good as ever.

On a serious level, middle age is a time when we recognize that we have already lived as many years—or more—as we have yet to live. In other words, we begin to realize for the first time that we are not going to live forever. We experience the death of young love and young dreams; we recognize that some of our goals are not going to be realized—or if we have reached our goals, we may become bored and ask, "Is this all there is?" Clare Boothe Luce once said, "Mid-life is the way you would feel about summer if you knew there would never be another spring."

In her best-selling book *Passages,* Gail Sheehy says that we will never navigate the midlife upheaval unless we have concomitant growth in three areas: our work; our relationships with significant others, such as spouses, children, and parents; and ourselves, or our personal development—mental, emotional, and spiritual. The great temptation is to become unbalanced—to give the vast majority of our energies to one of these areas and neglect the other two. Sheehy tells of a forty-year-old newscaster who had climbed to the top of his profession and was basking in the affluence and affirmation that went with being a national celebrity. He was not as satisfied, however, as we might suppose. He commented, "I am near the top of the mountain which I saw as a young man, but this is not snow up here; it's mostly salt." He said that most of the persons he knew who were considered successful had left their personal lives far behind. Professionally, they were terrific; but on a personal level, their lives were in disarray. What happened was that they quit growing personally and relationally when the crying ambition to succeed overtook them.

How do we navigate the stormy waters of midlife and come through to authenticity? In the story of the Velveteen Rabbit, the rabbit says to the Skin Horse, "Does it hurt to be real?" The horse replies: "Sometimes. Being real doesn't happen all at once. You become. It takes a long time. That's why it doesn't happen to people who break easily or have sharp edges or have to be carefully kept." How, then, does it happen? How do we become "real" through the midlife years? I believe that first and foremost, we must stay in close touch with Jesus Christ. In the Bible we read how David wandered away from God. It was only when he recognized his sin, repented, and returned to God that he was forgiven and could live a productive life. As the late Dr. E. Stanley

Jones once said, "By the time you reach forty, you ought to be reconverted [to Christianity] on general principles."

In addition to walking in daily fellowship with Christ, we must be sure we have completed the seasons of youth and young adulthood. As Paul writes in his first letter to the Corinthians, we must "put an end to childish ways" (13:11). This includes forgiving ourselves, our parents, and others we feel may have hurt us in some way. In order to do this, we must be able to acknowledge and express our feelings. Next, we must build an "adequate identity," a self-image based not on what we do but on who we are. Finally, we must form lasting friendships.

In his book *Halfway Up the Mountain*, David Morley writes:

> The Christian should not fear the middle passage of his life. He should view [it] as a time of enrichment. The flurry of youth is passed. His life begins to fall into step with reality.... He begins to enjoy the things that he has, rather than long for the things he cannot have. He begins to learn about patience and endurance. He does not continue in the unchecked appetites of youth. He accepts [responsibility for his life and is] no longer driven by every wind and doctrine. (Old Tappan, N.J.: Fleming H. Revell, 1979, p. 27)

So, the middle years can be a happy, productive transition rather than a traumatic time of crisis. The choice is ours!

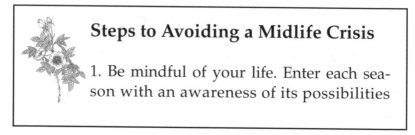

Steps to Avoiding a Midlife Crisis

1. Be mindful of your life. Enter each season with an awareness of its possibilities

and its pitfalls. Remember that *every* season of your life can be beautiful. Ecclesiastes 3:1 (NIV) tells us: "There is a time for everything, and a season for every activity under heaven: a time to be born and a time to die; a time to plant and a time to uproot."

2. Don't enter midlife before you have completed the seasons of youth and young adulthood. This means you must forgive yourself, your parents, and others you feel have hurt you in some way.

3. Learn to acknowledge and express your feelings.

4. Work intentionally on having an "adequate identity"—a self-image based not on what you do but on who you are!

5. Form a lasting friendship with at least one person of the same sex whom you can trust. Women seem to do this more easily than men, yet it is just as important to men. Every man needs to have at least one trusted male friend with whom he can share confidences and feelings.

6. Continue to grow in your work, your family relationships, and your own personal development—mental, emotional, and spiritual.

7. Set goals that will enable you to make the middle years a time of enrichment. Enjoy this period! Have fun with your family and learn to laugh at yourself.

8. Believe with Robert Browning that "the best is yet to be."

Chapter 13

Treat Loneliness Successfully

Remember, I am with you always, to the end of the age.
—*Matthew 28:20*

---

*I*t swept all over him. It was more enveloping than the darkness and more penetrating than the cold." These words were used by the English author Margaret Sangster to describe a five-year-old orphan in her book *The Littlest Orphan and the Christ Baby*. Although loneliness is characteristic of orphans and abused or neglected children, it is found in all ages and all socioeconomic groups. It is a universal experience. In fact, surveys have indicated that in our urban, technological society, loneliness has reached epidemic proportions. You can feel lonely in a crowd; you can feel lonely in a marriage in which there is turmoil and conflict; you can feel lonely when you are not included in an activity or even in a conversation.

Certainly you will feel lonely when you have gone through a painful separation—in a friendship, in a love relationship, in divorce, or in the loss of a loved one through death. A widow told me recently that 6:00 P.M. was the loneliest time of the day for her because that's when her husband usually came home from the office.

She said: "I used to wait for the sound of his key in the lock of our apartment. Now six o'clock comes, and there is no key in the lock, no familiar face, no one to cook dinner for. I'm so lonely I could die."

If loneliness is your problem, what can you do? First, be proactive. If you feel imprisoned by loneliness and would like to make a jail break, remember you are the jailer holding the key. Begin with your thoughts. If you see yourself as a lonely, almost friendless victim, you will live out that negative image. Instead, see yourself with a smile on your face and a song in your heart. Think of yourself inviting a friend to lunch or a movie or a concert. Think of yourself in church, meeting new friends. In other words, think of yourself as having a vital, interesting life. It was the late Dr. William James, a Harvard professor, who said that the most important discovery of his generation was that we can change our lives by changing our thoughts.

Second, remember that being alone doesn't have to mean being lonely. Learn to like yourself and to enjoy being alone, just as you enjoy being in the company of others. An article I read years ago has had a tremendous influence on my life. Though I have long since forgotten the name of the author, I have never forgotten its title: *You Become Someone Alone*. Neither have I forgotten the article's message. Basically, the author was saying that many things of significance and depth are best done alone, such as thinking, writing, composing, painting, organizing, writing letters, and so forth.

Third, get rid of the habits that are irritating to others. Many people are lonely because they turn people off. They may be irritable, rude, critical, self-centered, negative, opinionated, or just plain uninteresting. I know of a man who talks incessantly and is very opinionated. He never asks about other people's interests or opinions.

He doesn't listen, and he interrupts others when they are conversing. People avoid him like the plague. Is there any wonder why?

In addition to evaluating your habits, ask yourself how others see you. Do you smile readily or wear a frown? Do you stand confidently or slump dejectedly? Do you project cheerfulness and optimism or gloom and doom? Are you a fun person or a killjoy? In his poem "Myself," Edgar A. Guest expresses this need to like ourselves with these words:

> I have to live with myself, and so,
> I want to be fit for myself to know.

Fourth, replace self-pity and self-centeredness with a sincere interest in other people. When you respond to other people in genuine caring, it creates a state of harmony between you and others that is almost irresistible. We all need supportive relationships.

Once I heard Dr. Norman Vincent Peale say in a sermon that the giant redwood trees of California do not have deep roots as might be expected. Instead, they have a very shallow root system, designed to catch as much surface moisture as possible. And because the roots spread out in all directions, the roots of all the trees in a redwood grove are intertwined. They are locked together so that when the wind blows or a storm strikes, all the trees support and sustain one another. They need one another to survive. So do people!

Dr. Norman Neaves, pastor of the Church of the Servant in Oklahoma City, tells of receiving a letter from a parishioner who wanted to express appreciation for a regular part of the Sunday worship service. She wrote: "I live alone; I don't have any friends; and I am without a job. I guess you would say that I am very shy and not good at relating to people. This might be difficult for you to believe, Norman, but each Sunday when we hold hands and pray together the Lord's Prayer, it is the only time in the week when I touch someone or they touch me. I feel connected. I hope you won't ever stop doing that."

Finally, when you are feeling lonely, remember that you are never alone. A newspaper account of a power failure in Salt Lake City told of a hotel in which an elevator was stuck between floors in total darkness. Rescue workers heard a woman's voice inside and called out, "Are you alone?" She responded, "I am by myself, but I'm not alone." They knew that she meant God was with her.

Whether we are trapped in an elevator, separated from loved ones by distance or death, or rejected by others, we are not alone. Jesus said: "I am with you always, to the end of the age" (Matthew 28:20). Hold on to that assurance and let your loneliness fade away.

Steps to Overcoming Loneliness

1. Remember that loneliness is a universal problem and that you can overcome it by being proactive. Start by changing your thoughts. Instead of thinking of yourself as lonely, see yourself as having an interesting life. William James reminds us that "you can change your life by changing your thoughts."

2. Remember that being alone doesn't have to mean being lonely. Learn to like yourself and to enjoy being alone.

3. Get rid of habits that are irritating to others. In this way you can become a more likable person.

4. Replace self-centeredness with a sincere interest in others and develop a support system of friends.
5. Remember that you are never alone. Claim the promise of Matthew 28:20.

Chapter 14

Don't Play the "Blame Game"

The man said, "The woman whom you gave to be with me, she gave me fruit from the tree, and I ate."

—*Genesis 3:12*

I remember being treated to a fascinating study of human behavior. My husband and I were at the airport awaiting a flight to Grand Rapids, Michigan, to conduct a church consultation. As we waited in the gate area, we saw a man and woman dashing frantically through the terminal.

They were an attractive, physically fit, obviously affluent couple who looked as if they were in their early fifties. When they arrived at the gate, they had missed their flight to Miami. From their dress and conversation, we deducted that this was a crucial connection for a cruise to the Bahamas.

The door to the loading ramp was closed and locked; the agent had already left his position; and the plane, out on the tarmac, was revving its motors in preparation for takeoff.

The dark-haired woman beat on the locked glass door, demanding, "Open this door! We are about to miss our flight!" Of course, no one was outside to hear or respond. The man, displaying an intense facial expression, was obviously accustomed to being in charge. He picked up the telephone on the counter and attempted to call the check-in desk. "Send somebody down to gate 5 immediately or we will miss our flight." No response.

As the plane roared down the runway, the mutterings began. Though we caught only snatches of the couple's angry conversation, we heard the man say, "I told you not to have that second cup of coffee." To this, his wife retorted defiantly, "It's your fault. You never set the alarm early enough. You think people will always wait for you."

My heart felt sad as I saw two healthy, privileged adults, who I assumed had planned and paid for an exotic vacation, sabotage their situation by playing the age-old "blame game." People have been playing it since time began. When God called Adam and Eve to account for their disobedience, Adam blamed Eve and Eve blamed the serpent. Throughout the generations since, people have found it easy to indulge in this non-productive, destructive behavior.

Instead of taking responsibility for our lives, knowing that the consequences of our actions are the result of our own choices, we often try to hide behind silly reasoning, such as "I can't help getting angry; I have red hair"; "I'll never be good in math because my dad was never good at it, and I have deficient math genes"; or "No matter what I eat, I will always be fat; I come from a fat family." We've all heard people say such things as "You'd be the way I am if you had my lousy boss"; "My husband makes me so angry"; and "My children drive me crazy." Perhaps we've even said such things ourselves.

Constantly we must remind ourselves that we *choose* our feelings. No one can *make* us feel any particular way. It was former first lady Eleanor Roosevelt who said: "No one can make you feel inferior without your permission." And Gandhi—who almost single-handedly and without violence broke the caste system in India, paving the way for democracy and freedom—said, "They [the British] cannot take away our self-respect if we do not give it to them."

I am convinced that if we are to live freely, effectively, and creatively, then we must give up the "blame game" and take responsibility for our lives. How can we do this?

First, we need to remember that life is a precious gift from God. God not only gives us life but also offers to live it with us, if we will let him.

Second, we need to realize that we destroy our chance for abundant life when we hide behind others by blaming them. Since we have only one chance at life, and this is it, it doesn't make sense to waste it playing the blame game. As John Greenleaf Whittier says in his poem "Maud Muller," "For of all sad words of tongue or pen, The saddest are these: "It might have been!"

Third, we must recognize that our lives are the result of our choices. We all have certain genetic "limitations—irreversible characteristics such as the color of our eyes and hair, our height, the color of our skin, and so forth. We also have certain limitations or privileges according to our place of birth and the family into which we were born. Yet within those limitations, we determine what becomes of our lives.

Perhaps you are saying to yourself, "Wait a minute. I am in an impossible job situation. And because I need the money, I don't feel free to leave. I'm stuck!" Even in that situation, you have three choices: to leave, to stay and try to improve the situation, or to stay and change your attitude.

Fourth, we need to acknowledge that there are some situations over which we have no control, yet we must remember that how we respond in those situations is always our choice. For example, we might be involved in an accident, lose a loved one through death, or discover that we have a terminal illness. We would never choose any of these tragic situations. Yet in such situations, we have the ultimate freedom—the freedom to decide how we will react. We can choose to get bitter or better. Remember the wisdom of Austrian psychiatrist Viktor Frankl, who said that what happens to us is not nearly as important as how we react to what happens.

Fifth, and finally, we need to hear God speak to us as he did through Moses to the children of Israel in the wilderness: "I have set before you life and death, blessings and curses. Choose life" (Deuteronomy 30:19). Ultimately, the choice is ours.

Steps to Beating the "Blame Game"

1. Remember that life is a precious gift.
2. Realize that you destroy your chance for abundant living when you hide behind others by blaming them.
3. Recognize that your life is the result of your choices.
4. Fourth, acknowledge that there are some situations over which you have no control, but remember that how you respond in those situations is always your choice.
5. Hear God say to you, "I have set before you life and death, blessings and curses. Choose life" (Deuteronomy 30:19).

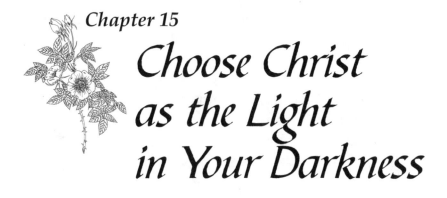

Chapter 15

Choose Christ as the Light in Your Darkness

Trust in the LORD with all your heart, and lean not on your own understanding.

—Proverbs 3:5 NIV

W hen I answered the telephone, the voice at the other end said, "Nell, can you stop by my house today? I have something to share with you."

"Yes," I answered, "I'd love to. I will be there around three o'clock this afternoon."

When I placed the receiver back on the hook, I thought about my friend Helen who had called. Five years had passed since she had been hospitalized after a nervous breakdown, and she now had resumed many of her activities. *Is there any possibility that Helen will tell me something of the feelings she experienced during the dark night of her spirit?* I wondered hopefully. She did!

As the warm sunlight filtered into her attractively appointed living room, Helen told the poignant story of her breakdown. With no hesitancy of speech, she spoke of life in happier days, admitting that she always had been a perfectionist. This is what she told me:

I liked everything clean and in order—the children, the house, the schedule. My husband, Jim, traveled much of the week, and I had most of the responsibility for the children. Jim, however, was always available by telephone and in person when I needed him.

We had the usual ups and downs of rearing children, but nothing we couldn't control. Basically, we were an active, happy, church-going family. Then, in a period of six years, five events occurred over which I had no control. First was the death of my father from leukemia; then the unexpected heart attack and death of my youngest sister; followed by the lingering illness and death of my brother, my father-in-law, and my mother. These events happened so quickly that I was emotionally numb, unable to express the grief I felt. In retrospect, I realize that for six years I had felt torn between my responsibility to care for my aging, senile mother and my responsibility for my husband and children.

Slowly a feeling of great anxiety began to hang over me like a terrible weight. My body felt heavy, and claustrophobic fears appeared. For instance, I found it almost impossible to ride in the car with other people unless the windows were down, providing a way of escape. I dreaded going into public restrooms because you had to lock the door, and that made me feel trapped, caged. More and more I wanted to withdraw.

The event that finally sent me to a psychiatric hospital was a small thing that happened with one of our college-age children. It assumed unrealistic proportions in my mind, causing me to lose all perspective. When my husband came home from a business trip, he found me sitting in a darkened room, telling the story of the incident over and over again. Though I was unaware of it, none of the housework had been done. I simply had lost my ability to cope with everyday living.

Recognizing that I was in trouble, Jim called our doctor. He suggested immediate hospitalization. In my distorted mind, I thought I had somehow offended two of my best friends, and I insisted that Jim invite them to come over so that I could apologize. Feeling that they might help persuade me to go to the hospital, he invited them. The next thirty minutes were terrible. I was angry and completely bewildered by the fact that my husband and best friends wanted me to go to the hospital when I didn't need to go. When none of their persuasion worked, my husband picked me up bodily and put me in the car. Though angry and argumentative throughout the ride, I didn't attempt to escape from the car.

After Jim checked me into the hospital, the doctor suggested that Jim leave. I was given some forms to fill out. I refused to fill them out; I refused to eat; I refused to go to bed. At about 11:30 P.M., I was seated at a long table, fully clothed, still looking at the forms. I knew I needed help and began to make a list of people who might help me. First, I listed my husband, but then I marked through his name. Then I listed my son and daughter, but I marked through their names. The names of close friends were methodically marked through. Finally, and almost as if the name were written by someone beyond myself, I printed the letters J E S U S.

This time, instead of marking through the name, I circled it. A feeling of assurance permeated my body like a warm current of electricity. Suddenly I knew that I would receive help, and I knew the source of it. Tears of gratitude fell like hot rain from my tired eyes. I went to bed and slept soundly.

After six weeks in the hospital, I returned home with hope and a bottle of tranquilizers. From time to time, I returned to the hospital on an out-patient basis to talk with the psychiatrist. Because the tranquilizers had helped me to function, I was afraid to stop taking them. A year and a half later, I was still taking the tranquilizers—functioning, yes, but feeling and acting like a zombie. One beautiful spring afternoon, I walked out onto the back porch and, watching a squirrel scamper playfully across the yard, I asked myself, "Will I ever be free again? Can I be fully well?"

The words that came in reply I heard within my mind, but from beyond myself. I firmly believe that they were the words of God pointing me to freedom. "Throw the pills away!" was the firm command. Without hesitation, I walked inside and flushed the contents of a half-full bottle down the commode. When I told the doctor what I had done, he replied that the pills were not addictive, so I should have no withdrawal symptoms. He was right. Within twenty-four hours my mind began to clear, and I felt I was reentering the land of the living.

Helen's eyes sparkled as she concluded her story: "I am grateful to all of the doctors and nurses who helped me in my recovery, and to my family for their support; but I know that my real help in healing came from the Great Physician, Jesus Christ."

Later, as I thought of our conversation, I realized that Helen had returned from a journey into nowhere. For her, the nowhere was a nervous breakdown, but for us, it could be one of many other things—marital problems, the rebellion of a child, betrayal by a friend, a seemingly impossible work situation, deep loneliness. Helen's road back, which I have outlined as part of the following steps to overcoming depression, can point the way for each of us, too. Remember, Jesus is ready and waiting to help!

Steps to Overcoming Depression

1. Recognize and analyze your problem. Early signs of depression include the inability to relax, a tendency to feel "blue," a change in sleep patterns—insomnia or the desire to sleep more—feelings of irritation, a change in eating patterns, and a growing dependence on stimulants. Schedule a physical checkup—to be sure that you do not have some kind of physical imbalance—and discuss such problems with your doctor.

2. Write down the names of other people who may be able to help—and/or places where you can go for help.

3. *Follow through* on seeking help.

4. In addition to taking any medication prescribed by your doctor, be diligent about eating a healthy diet. Eat lean meat and plenty of complex carbohydrates, vegetables, and fruits. Use caffeine and refined sugar sparingly, or not at all.

5. Exercise daily. It is especially important to walk in the out-of-doors. Moving our muscles helps to relieve anxiety, and being in nature calms our spirits.

6. Take "mini-vacations" throughout your day when you breathe deeply, relax your body (directions for this can be found in *Relaxation Response* by Herbert Benson), picture a peaceful place, and quiet your mind by saying biblical affirmations such as these:

- "In quietness and in confidence shall be your strength" (Isaiah 30:15 KJV).
- "Be still, and know that I am God!" (Psalm 46:10).
- "They that wait upon the LORD shall renew their strength" (Isaiah 40:31 KJV).
- "For God hath not given us the spirit of fear; but of power, and of love, and of a sound mind" (2 Timothy 1:7 KJV).

7. Listen to quiet music and pray before going to sleep.

8. At the start of each new day, choose Jesus! Practice daily what the scripture says: "Trust in the LORD with all your heart, and do not rely on your own insight. In all your ways acknowledge him, and he will make straight your paths" (Proverbs 3:5-6).

Chapter 16

Watch Your Reactions

[When the Samaritan village rejects Jesus, the disciples ask] Lord, do you want us to command fire to come down from heaven and consume them?

—Luke 9:54

"What happens to you in life is not nearly as important as how you react to what happens." The speaker at my high school graduation said these words, and this quotation has been locked in my mind ever since. It has helped guide me through the ups and downs, the detours and the unexpected turns of my life. My experience has proved that the speaker was right on target. I have used that quotation in all the ages and stages of my earthly journey, and I have seen its truth in the lives of others.

I once met two middle-aged women in the Milwaukee suburb of Whitefish Bay. They grew up in that affluent suburb and attended the same schools, including the University of Wisconsin. Both were active members in the same church. These two women had even experienced similar difficulties—serious health problems, the death of a spouse, and reduced income. Yet their perceptions of and attitudes toward life were diametrically opposite.

One woman, though she continued to function in her

daily activities, had put her life in a holding pattern. Like an airplane having to circle the airport because of landing problems, this woman was going around in circles, seemingly unwilling to "land" and move in a different direction. Because she refused to turn her past difficulties loose, she was bitter, critical of others, and unable to make objective, unemotional decisions. She was full of self-pity. All conversation with her eventually led to a discussion of the difficult circumstances of her life.

Her friend, on the other hand, who has felt the losses in her life just as keenly, has grieved in healthy ways. With God's help—and her faith intact—she consciously took her life off "hold." After receiving some additional education, she reentered the workforce. Through it all she did not blame others for her difficulties. She told me that she believed when Jesus said "In this world you will have trouble" (John 16:33 NIV), he was speaking to all of us. As she explained it, we are not supposed to "wallow" in our troubles. She said, "God gives us the power to overcome and move on, but we have to make the first move."

It was very obvious that the two women created opposite climates. The first was a negative, bitter climate, but the second was a happy, "can do" climate. What caused the difference? Obviously, the temperaments and circumstances of the two women were slightly different, but the second woman's climate was positive mainly because she chose to make it that way. She knew that "what happens to you in life is not nearly as important as how you react to what happens." She learned to focus on possibilities and alternatives rather than problems. She faced the future instead of the past. She chose to be proactive rather than reactive. Even her language was proactive.

Reactive language sounds something like this: "There is nothing I can do about this"; "That's just the way I am"; "That makes me so mad." Proactive language, on the other hand, sounds like this: "Let's look at the alternatives"; "I can choose a different approach"; "I can control my own feelings."

Several years ago, a friend of mine was dying of cancer. She was totally proactive in the freedoms she exercised by choosing how she would react to her imminent death. She chose not to take most of the pain medication so that she could interact with her husband and children. She used her failing strength to dictate notes that would be given to her children at significant events in her lives. Her influence for good will go on in the lives of her family because she chose to make it so.

Our attitudes affect our perceptions of life. Proactive people see life as a wonderful gift and choose to enjoy the gift. Proactive people appreciate beauty in the physical world. How can anyone see the beauty of the world in its changing seasons and not rejoice? Proactive people also see beauty in the people around them and never take others for granted. If we can enjoy the people we love in the here and now, we won't suffer the terrible regrets that come to those who focus only on ambition or are preoccupied with business or trivia.

Two other qualities characterized the happy, positive woman I met in Whitefish Bay. One was a good sense of humor. This happy lady laughed easily and often. Though she was serious about life and her job, she did not take herself too seriously. In other words, she was not self-centered. This enabled her to have a much clearer perspective on life. The other quality was a deeply rooted faith in God—a willingness to trust in God's resources. Her faith enabled her to stay anchored when life's difficulties occurred. It provided her with an inner gyroscope that righted her life after she was pushed down.

Remember, the doors to faith and change are locked on the inside. God offers us the strength to open the doors, but *we* have to turn the lock!

Steps to Becoming *Pro*active Rather than *Re*active

1. Remember that Jesus told us we will have trouble in this life. Instead of asking "Why me?" ask "Why not me?" After all, our lives also are filled with God's blessings. We never seem to question when something good happens to us.

2. Stay close to the Power Source. God's grace can comfort you and give you the power to go on, but you have to *receive* that power. For me, God's power comes through the Scriptures, prayer, quiet listening, worship, and holy communion.

3. After you move through the necessary grief stages, ask the question that Saul asked on the road to Damascus: "Lord, what [will you] have me to do?" (Acts 9:6 KJV). Listen for answers and watch for doors to open.

4. Listen to your "self-talk." Be sure that it is proactive instead of reactive.

5. Use Philippians 4:13 as a daily affirmation: "I can do all things through [Christ] who strengthens me." Don't just say it; believe it and act on it!

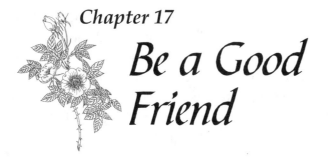

Chapter 17

Be a Good Friend

Be hospitable to one another without complaining.

—*1 Peter 4:9*

On a television program several years ago, George Burns was asked about his friendship with the late Jack Benny. He replied: "Jack and I were friends for fifty-five years. He never walked out on me when I sang, and I never walked out on him when he played his violin. We talked to each other almost every day of those fifty-five years. We had a wonderful friendship."

As I recall that comment, I think of another well-known friendship, the story of which was later depicted in the movie *Brian's Song*. It is the story of a friendship between two professional football players, Brian Piccolo and Gale Sayers. Brian—or "Pick" as he was called—developed cancer and was hospitalized. Gale would often finish a football game and then fly to Pick's bedside to offer encouragement and support.

There was a short time when Pick seemed better, and the two men and their wives planned to attend the national sportswriters' dinner in New York City, where Gale was to receive the George C. Halas Award for the most courageous player of the year.

When the day arrived, however, Pick was back in the hospital and critically ill. When accepting the award that night in New York, Gale said in a sincere and moving manner: "I accept this award on behalf of my friend, Brian Piccolo. He is the most courageous player." Then, in a voice shaking with emotion, he added, "When you hit your knees tonight, I hope that you will ask God to bless him."

Friendship is one of life's greatest treasures. The truth of this statement was reinforced for me after a recent visit with our good friends Witt and Helen Langstaff. Through the years my husband and I have visited the Langstaffs, and we have never left them without feeling better about life and personally refreshed—physically, mentally, and spiritually. They truly have the gift of hospitality.

What comprises hospitality and friendship? When I think of the Langstaffs, I think of several attributes. First, they are people whose lives are centered in important spiritual values—faith, family, friends, church, and community. As a result, they are comfortable with themselves and can accept other people as they are. As a guest in their home, I never feel I have to strive to "measure up" or fit into anyone else's mold. I am free to be myself. I'm convinced that God loves us that way. God accepts us "warts and all"; and in our acceptance through Christ, God releases us to be more than we have been.

Second, there is a "sparkle" in their friendship. Like the buildup on fine furniture that makes the finish sparkle, there is a buildup of little acts of thoughtfulness and kindness that make a friendship sparkle. The Langstaffs are masters at this—putting bouquets of freshly picked flowers in our room; remembering to leave onions, to which my husband is allergic, out of the salad; sending notes and pictures of events we have shared.

Third, they use the tools of affirmation and praise to create the climate of hospitality. Their subtle compliments, sincerely given, leave you with the feeling of being special. They have used these tools in the rearing of their five fine children, and now they are using them with their grandchildren, all of whom come home for regular visits. In addition, they enable their grandchildren to feel special by having each child come for a week's visit when he or she turns eight. From a list of suggested activities, the grandchild chooses what he or she would most like to do.

Fourth, they are positive, joyful people, which makes their home a place you like to be. Instead of whining and complaining, they substitute good humor, laughter, and caring. They express this caring in many ways. One way is by listening attentively as you speak and asking questions that show their interest and support. Another way is freely expressing their affection with words such as, "We're so glad you are here," "We've missed you," and "We value your friendship."

An indication of the flexibility and versatility of the Langstaffs' hospitality is the number of foreign students and visitors who have been their houseguests. Surely these guests' impression of the United States is that of a gentle, kind nation because of the warm hospitality they have experienced in the Langstaffs' home.

Yes, friendship is one of life's greatest treasures, and hospitality is the crowning gift of friendship. Through hospitality we open our homes and hearts to our friends and others who need us. The Bible says that hospitality is an evidence of God's presence within (Romans 12:13). Do others see this evidence of God in you?

Steps to Being a Good Friend

1. Value your friends. We live in a world that uses and discards relationships with the same ease that we discard cars and freezers, but God didn't create us to be Lone Rangers. Even the Lone Ranger had Tonto.

2. Remember that you need to have friendships in three levels or categories: casual relationships (people to whom we say "hello"); good relationships (friends with whom we go places and do things); and close relationships (people we love and trust, and with whom we share our dreams, hopes, and fears).

3. In the category of close relationships, let Christ's relationship with his twelve disciples be your model.

• He accepted them despite their differences.

• He encouraged them. An example is when he called Peter a "rock" long before Peter was a rock. By that act, he liberated Peter to become more than he was.

• He spent time with them. They traveled together, ate together, laughed together. We can't be casual about close relationships; we must take time to "be there" in the joys and in the sorrows.

• He had "care-frontations" with them, such as when James and John asked to sit one at his left hand and one at his right hand in his kingdom. Jesus helped them to see a bigger picture. We can disagree with our close friends in love.

• He was full of joy so that they enjoyed being with him. Even as he faced his death, he said: "I have said these things to you so that my joy may be in you, and that your joy may be complete" (John 15:11).

Chapter 18

Be Up on Down Days

I lift up my eyes to the hills—from where will my help come? My help comes from the LORD, who made heaven and earth.

—Psalm 121:1-2

Some days you just don't want to get out of bed! You're facing a horrendous schedule, or you have a responsibility that you are not sure how to handle, or you know that you will be meeting a difficult person. You feel "down."

I had such a day not long ago. When I awakened, my sinuses were swollen from allergies, which caused me to have a sinus headache. In addition, I was facing some responsibilities that I hadn't decided exactly how to handle, and indecision always makes me tired. Yet the alarm was ringing. It was time to get up. I put one foot on the floor, and the other said, "I'm not coming!"

I knew I needed to remember the formula I had worked out for how to be up on down days. It has six steps. Perhaps they can be of some help to you, too, on "down" days.

First, start the day positively. The cynic W. C. Fields used to advise people to smile first thing in the morning and get it over with. By starting the day positively, I mean something far deeper than that. As I've suggested in previous chapters, if I condition my mind with gratitude when I awaken, I set my direction for the day—accentuating blessings and possibilities rather than problems.

Second, treat your body to "high octane gasoline." Twenty minutes of vigorous exercise (each day, if possible, or at least three times a week) and a high-fiber, low-fat diet gives us the best fuel for our physical bodies. Likewise, thirty minutes or more of quiet time for reading inspirational literature, including the Bible, thinking, and praying provide the best fuel for our minds and spirits. I have learned that the answer to a problem I have been wrestling with often becomes crystal clear when I am quiet, calm, and prayerful.

Third, remember that you can think your way through any difficulty or problem—but you must *think*, not *react* emotionally. It is such a temptation to react in fear, anger, or pettiness. We have achieved a great skill when we can discipline ourselves to be calm when faced with problems. I have found that when I center myself in quietness, it is the Holy Spirit that calms my spirit, often bringing to my remembrance a Bible verse or the words of a reassuring hymn. So often I recall this verse from the hymn "Dear Lord and Father of Mankind," written by John Greenleaf Whittier in 1872:

> Drop thy still dews of quietness,
> Till all our strivings cease;
> Take from our souls the strain and stress,
> And let our ordered lives confess
> The beauty of thy peace.

Fourth, stop thinking "what if . . . ?" "What if I forget my speech?" "What if I fail?" "What if they don't like me?" "What if I get fired?" "What if I have a tumor?" "What if it is malignant?" The list goes on and on. Focus, instead, on how you are going to handle the problem. Don't run away from it, and don't procrastinate. Face your fear and determine how you can best solve it.

Fifth, cut your problem down to size. Take it apart, break it into its components, and tackle each of those components one at a time. Once I heard Jill Briscoe, Christian author and speaker, tell of being over-whelmed by a cluttered, junk-filled garage that needed to be cleaned out. Because it was such a gigantic job, she kept postponing it until a neighbor said, "Jill, all you have to do is to clean up one corner at a time." That bit of advice has helped me tackle problems that seemed too big to be conquered.

Sixth, believe that "when God closes a door, he always opens a window." These were the words of Mother Superior to Maria in the movie *The Sound of Music.* It is a reminder that there are opportunities in every problem. For one thing, trouble makes us more understanding. You can't understand what it's like to have children in difficulty until you have children in difficulty. You don't understand what it's like to lose a spouse unless this has happened to you. I firmly believe there is nothing that can happen to us that we and God together cannot handle.

That's my formula for being up on down days. I challenge you to try it!

Steps for Being Up on Down Days

1. When you awaken in the morning, instead of thinking about how much you have to do, condition your mind with gratitude.

2. Give your body "high octane gasoline" through regular exercise and a nutritious diet. It's especially important to eat a good breakfast. You wouldn't put inferior gasoline into an expensive new car. Your body will last much longer than your car, and it is far more valuable to you!

3. Learn to think through problems and difficulties, rather than react emotionally.

4. Stop thinking "what if . . . ?" Instead, focus on how you are going to handle your problem or fear.

5. Cut your problems down to size and tackle one component at a time.

6. Remember that God always provides options and opportunities, and choose to live in God's power!

Chapter 19

Grow a Strong Marriage

[Love] bears all things, believes all things, hopes all things, and endures all things. Love never ends.

—1 Corinthians 13:7-8a

They looked too young to be getting married. Yet that was merely my perception, because they both had graduated from college, they had dated for four years, they had similar backgrounds, and each had a job. In today's world, those are strong indicators for an enduring marriage.

The bride, with bouncy blonde hair and dancing brown eyes, looked radiant as she walked down the aisle on the arm of her father. The six-foot-two-inch groom, with serious blue eyes, smiled as he waited for his bride at the altar. The organist was playing "Trumpet Voluntaire," and everyone was smiling. Why, then, was I feeling anxiety?

Maybe it was because I have seen too many young people stand at the altar with dreams in their hearts only to have those dreams become nightmares later, eventually taking them to divorce court. Or maybe it was because the "rules" seem to have changed since I stood at the altar so many years ago. Indeed, the American family has been reinvented since the early fifties. Many of the changes are welcome and wonderful, but some impose heavy pressures on young marriages.

Yet there are some things that never change. There are principles upon which all long-lasting relationships are built. It was an understanding of these principles that I wished for the young bride and groom at the wedding I attended. It is the same understanding I wish for all couples planning to be married, as well as those who have been married for years—whatever their ages or circumstances.

The first principle is that you *grow* a strong marriage. It doesn't just happen. One of the most important "growth ingredients" is choosing a partner whose character you can trust. Commitment is another necessary ingredient. In a day when "quick fixes" are popular and appealing, some people "trade in" their spouses for a "newer model" with the ease of a new car transaction. Don't buy into that kind of mentality. Determine early to work through your differences and difficulties "for better, for worse; in sickness and in health."

After you are married, you need to put preventive measures into effect immediately, but it is never too late to begin using these measures. One preventive measure is to keep romance alive and continue to show affection and appreciation. Don't ever take each other for granted. Instead, always respect your spouse as a person of worth; that includes his or her feelings, thoughts, and opinions. Take time to listen, to care, to encourage, and to celebrate.

One of the terrific pressures on young couples and families today is lack of time. With both spouses working in many cases, and with each participating in church, civic, and social activities—especially later as children arrive—two people can easily grow in different directions. Don't let this happen! Plan to "neglect" or postpone other activities so that you may take time regularly for the two of you—time when you may dream together, laugh together, and enjoy activities together that will enrich and strengthen your marriage. When you do this, you not only experience happiness in the present, but you also "build" happiness for the future—including your retirement years!

Another preventive measure is to decide how you will handle conflict. There is no doubt about it: You *will* disagree. I love the quotation attributed to Mrs. Billy Graham: "When two people agree all the time about everything, one of them is unnecessary." The way you handle conflict may determine whether or not your marriage will hold together or come apart at the seams.

Although every couple must work out their own methods for handling conflict creatively, I'd like to share a couple of things I've learned in the process. First, no one has to "win" an argument. You both may be right, and certainly you both need to be heard before compromises are worked out. In fact, the four words "you may be right" can actually disarm an argument. The minister who performed the marriage ceremony for my husband and me gave us some good biblical advice: "Do not let the sun go down on your anger" (Ephesians 4:26). In other words, "Don't go to bed angry." Later I told the minister that we stayed up later that first year of marriage than ever before. But it certainly got us in the habit of talking through our problems and finding a mutually satisfying solution.

Praying together is another excellent method for handling conflict. It is hard to talk to God in your spouse's presence and still be mad at your spouse. Forgiveness is truly the glue that holds your relationship together.

The second principle for growing a strong marriage is learn to enjoy the present. Many couples plan to be happy "when . . . "—when they can own a house, buy a new car, take a great vacation, have children, get the children into school, or get the children through college. They are always planning to be happy in the future. My advice is to celebrate today! Don't miss the moment or ruin it by being unhappy about what you don't have yet.

This is a good time to say a special word about children, for they are grown and gone before we know it. Welcome each one when he or she is born, whether planned or unplanned. There is nothing sadder in this world than children who are not wanted and know it. They become the depressed or angry young people who never quite find their niche in life. When we come to the end of our days, my guess is that every accomplishment we have achieved will pale in comparison to the privilege of being cocreators with God. Having and rearing whole persons in the family will be our finest accomplishments.

So, celebrate each day! Celebrate birthdays and "unbirthdays"; celebrate promotions and nonpromotions; celebrate your spouse and your children. Celebrate life!

The third principle for growing a strong marriage is to live for something bigger than yourself or your spouse. Marriage was God's idea. I've always been thankful that God didn't have us live as lonely, alienated human beings. Instead, God placed us in families so that we may give and receive love, security, faith, and hope for the future. When this happens, the family becomes a microcosm of God's plan for the world—or the "kingdom of God," as Jesus called it. The couple who establish their marriage on the purposes of God, enrich their marriage by attending church regularly, and reach beyond themselves to serve others will build a home that is a haven of peace and a blessing to those who experience it.

In this exciting time of change and opportunity, we need lots of marriages built on the foundation of these three principles!

Steps to Growing a Strong Marriage

1. Remember that a strong marriage doesn't just happen. You have to grow one, which requires time and effort.

2. Choose a partner whose character you can trust, for commitment is a necessary ingredient for a strong, lasting marriage.

3. Don't even think about divorce; instead, think and work toward a lifelong relationship.

4. Build into your marriage some preventive measures, such as keeping romance alive; continuing to show affection and appreciation; and taking time to listen, to care, to encourage, and to celebrate.

5. Learn to handle conflict creatively. Remember, no one has to "win" an argument.

6. Pray together. Remember that forgiveness is the glue that holds your relationship together.

7. Enjoy the present. Don't just plan to be happy "when. . . ." You have this moment. Celebrate it!

8. Welcome your children when they are born and continue to celebrate them.

9. Make your home a "haven of peace" by establishing your marriage on the purposes of God, attending church regularly, and reaching beyond yourselves to serve others.

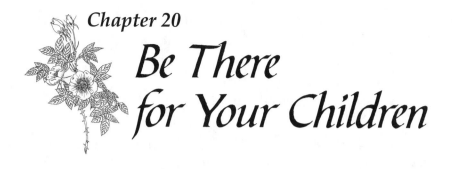

Chapter 20

Be There for Your Children

Do not provoke your children to anger, but bring them up in the discipline and instruction of the Lord.

—Ephesians 6:4

*T*he sky is falling, Henny Penny!" That was the opening line of the "Chicken Little" drama presented by the kindergarten children on the final day of Girls Preparatory School summer camp. Surrounded by Ducky Lucky, Foxy Loxy, Goosey Lucy, and the other barnyard characters, my granddaughter, Ellen, gave a stellar performance as Turkey Lurkey.

Of course, every parent or grandparent present experienced the same feelings of pride about their children and grandchildren. As I looked around the theater, I was instantly aware of two things. First, I was impressed by the number of men and women who had left their places of work to see the charming but somewhat unpolished performance. Second, I was impressed by the tremendous amount of love and affirmation that flowed from the audience to the juvenile performers on the stage.

To the casual observer, this may seem an insignificant incident. Perhaps there are those who feel it is a waste of important business time to attend such a function. But the parents and grandparents who were there knew that they were making wonderful memories. Far more important than the money, furniture, or silver we may leave our children are the memories, the ideals, and the values we pass on to them. This is the stuff a good life is made of.

At the performance that day, those parents and grandparents added another block in the foundation of their child's or grandchild's self-esteem. It is a wonderful thing for children to feel that they are important enough to be listened to, loved, and appreciated by the significant adults in their lives. In ten to fifteen years, the children who performed that day may say to their friends something like this: "When I look back on my life, I realize that my family came to even the smallest things that I did and cheered me on."

Recently I had the opportunity to talk with a girl whose parents have never "been there" for her. Chari is a pretty teenager, but she is insecure and unsure of herself, and she has an inordinate need for affection. I have known her parents for a long span of years. They are not bad people. In fact, they are pleasant, entertaining people whom you would enjoy if you met them socially. They both are attractive, bright, and very successful professionally. They enjoy people, travel, and social activities.

Though Chari's parents sincerely love her, their lives are so "full" that there seems to be no time to do anything with their daughter. Certainly, there is not time to leave their professions in the middle of the day to see her perform in a school play or to watch her on the soccer field. The time she needs to talk to them about something seems invariably to be when they are on their way out of town or to an important social event.

It isn't that Chari's parents haven't provided for her

financially or educationally. She attends the best private school, lives in a lovely home, has beautiful clothes, and gets a larger allowance than her friends. Unfortunately, however, they have not provided the emotional and spiritual values so necessary for the greening of the human spirit.

Even as I write this, I am aware that some deeply caring parents find it impossible to leave their jobs to attend their children's activities. These parents, however, find the time after work to listen, to talk, and most important, to care. I also know that doing everything possible to affirm and support our children doesn't necessarily mean that they will turn out well. There comes a time when a young person decides for himself or herself which way to go in life. Just as we cannot choose the road our children will take in life, so also we cannot choose all the "furniture" for their "life houses." Peers, teachers, and circumstances will help to determine this. Yet we parents and grandparents do have the privilege and responsibility of building a solid foundation of emotional wholeness for each human life entrusted to us. To build this foundation we need three building blocks: unconditional love, discipline, and faith.

Unconditional love means love with no strings attached. We don't say by our words or actions, "We love you . . . if you are good"; "We love you . . . if you make good grades"; or "We love you . . . if you do what we tell you to do." Rather, we say, "We love you because you are you and because you are part of this family." There is no security in the whole world like that.

The word *discipline* comes from the root word meaning "to teach." Discipline means teaching our children values and the important difference between right and wrong. It involves giving them guidance and direction. Perhaps all of us need to be reminded that this guidance should come through our example as well as our words. As Ralph Waldo Emerson wrote, "Do not say things. What you are stands over you the while, and thunders so that I cannot hear what you say to the contrary."

Finally, there's *faith*. I believe the greatest gift we can give our children is to place their hands into the hand of God. We can't always be there with them, but God can. Our love and wisdom are limited, but God's aren't. It will be this personal experience of faith that will provide the framework for our children's character and value system, which they will use as they live out the rest of their lives.

When speaking to the Council of Bishops of The United Methodist Church in 1999, Bishop Kenneth Carder asked this disturbing question: "Is there enough evidence to convict The United Methodist Church of child neglect?" As families, we must ask ourselves the same question. Despite the busyness and fragmentation of our days, we must make building a strong foundation for our children one of our top priorities.

 Steps to "Being There" for Your Children

1. Give your children unconditional love. Your words and actions should say "I love you because you are you and you are part of this family." There is no security in the whole world like that.
2. Remember that touch is important in communicating love. In her book *Peoplemaking,* Virginia Satir says that children need four hugs a day just to keep them functioning, eight hugs a day to give them

---

self-esteem, and twelve hugs a day to keep them at the peak of well-being.

3. One of the greatest gifts you can give your children is to enjoy them. Let them know that they are not a burden but a joy.

4. Make a commitment to be present as often as possible for their activities.

5. Have fun together as a family.

6. It is your responsibility to teach your children the difference between right and wrong. You should not only teach values but also exemplify them.

7. Put your children's hands into the hands of God. Take them to Sunday school and church, and live the Christian faith joyfully before them. Remember Proverbs 22:6: "Train children in the right way, and when old, they will not stray."

Chapter 21

Enjoy Grandparenting

I am reminded of your sincere faith, a faith that lived first in your grandmother Lois and your mother Eunice and now, I am sure, lives in you.

—*2 Timothy 1:5*

---

*H*ow do you spell fatigue? If you are my age, you spell it DISNEY WORLD, especially if you have two grandchildren who are human versions of the Energizer Bunny—they keep going and going. Actually, we had three long, hot, fun-filled days at Disney World, but by the time our plane touched down at the Chattanooga airport on our return trip, every bone in my body ached. Yet I wouldn't take anything for the memory of those days. The memories are better than Bengay for alleviating the pain!

This adventure happened because my husband and I were in Orlando attending a leadership conference. Since the conference ended on Wednesday at noon, we decided to invite our grandchildren—who at that time were ages eleven and eight—to fly down and be our guests for two and a half days at Disney World. Their prompt response to our invitation was, "Yes! Yes! Yes!"

The following are some of the lessons I learned from the unlikely pairing of the old and the young at such a vast and spectacular theme park. First, children are extremely energized and motivated—getting up early, dressing, and picking up the room—when there's something they really want to do. But adults are the same. Have you ever had a project at work that so engaged and excited you that you worked long hours and still felt energized? This is why it is necessary to discover our unique talents and, if possible, to find a vocation in which those talents can be utilized. If not in a vocation, then certainly in an avocation or volunteer job. Likewise, as motivators and employers, we can help others match their talents with appropriate tasks.

Second, there always will be tedious chores that we have to do in order to enjoy the more pleasant ones. At the Enclave Suites where we stayed in Orlando, we had four rules: (1) keep all your belongings off the floor and put them where they belong, (2) have fun, (3) have fun, and (4) have fun. The first rule didn't seem so hard to Ellen and Wesley when they could look forward to the other three!

On Wednesday, soon after our grandchildren bounced off the plane, we took them to "Wet and Wild," a huge water park near the Magic Kingdom and only a block from our motel. We laughingly said that they were wet and we were wild—running from one attraction to another. In addition to small and giant water slides of many varieties, there were attractions such as a lazy river for floating in "tubes," a pool of waves to "ride," plenty of entertainment, and lots of junk food. The lesson I learned from the water park was that nobody looks good when they are "all wet." In fact, when we left late that evening, we all dragged out of the park looking like drowned rats.

Similarly, whether the setting is work, home, or a social gathering, people who are "all wet" are not a sight for sore eyes. In fact, they are a pain to be around. They have a negative attitude, they complain, and they throw "cold water" on new ideas or projects. Generally, they make no positive contributions whatsoever. It's one thing to be all wet at a water park; but in daily life, we need to keep our attitudes "high and dry."

Since the children had been to the Magic Kingdom a number of times with their parents, they chose carefully how we would spend the short period of time we had there. On Thursday, we spent the entire day at Disney World. I never enter the Magic Kingdom without being impressed anew with three things: the cleanliness of the grounds, the courtesy of the staff, and most of all, the creative genius of Walt Disney. Just think: It all began when he created a mouse named Mickey! As I experienced once again the beauty and fantasy of the Magic Kingdom, I thought how each of us has the ability to be creative. In fact, according to research findings I once read, all of us can be more creative than we are now if we will work to develop our right-brain thinking.

Though we watched the parade on Main Street and had dinner there, we spent most of our time in Frontier Land and Tomorrow Land. The children enjoyed many rides, but their favorite was Splash Mountain. Based on Walt Disney's 1946 film *Song of the South*, Splash Mountain boasts one of the world's tallest and sharpest flume drops—standing fifty-two and a half feet at a forty-five degree angle, with a top speed of forty miles an hour. After hurtling down Chickapin Hill, the eight-passenger log boat hits the pond below with a giant splash and then promptly sinks underwater, or so it seems, with only a trace of bubbles left in its wake.

As we traveled by skyway on the WEDway people-mover from one event to another, all four of us enjoyed such attractions as Mission to Mars, Carousel of Progress, Dream Flight, and Circlevision. Finally, I got nerve enough to join the children on Space Mountain, which is

Disney's version of a roller-coaster—and then some! The ride takes place in outer-spacelike darkness that gets progressively blacker and scarier as the journey progresses. The children kept looking back at me in our three-passenger rocket and calling out, "Open your eyes, Gran!" When we finally climbed out of our spaceship, I staggered around like a drunken person until I got my land legs again. As I walked on to the next attraction, my silent prayer was, "Lord, if I have courage enough to do this crazy thing, let me always have courage enough to stand firm on important moral issues in a crazy, mixed up world."

For our final day, we chose Universal Studios. It was a delightful choice, featuring everything from Nickelodeon Studios, to Ghostbusters, to a "Back to the Future" blastoff on an unbelievable twenty-one million zigowatt adventure, to a simulated earthquake (8.3 on the Richter scale and 10 on the scale of fun). In Kongfrontation, King Kong trapped us in a cable car high above the East River. And at E.T. Adventure, we hopped aboard starbound bikes and raced across the moon to save E.T.'s dying planet. That adventure had a memorable ending, with E.T. waving good-bye and calling each of us by name.

Animal actors such as Lassie, Bengie, Beethoven, and Mister Ed, the talking horse, gave an hour's unforgettable performance. Then there was the Wild, Wild, Wild West Show, which featured stunts you could see but could hardly believe.

I came away from the imaginative wonders of that day thinking of these lines from Robert Louis Stevenson's poem "Happy Thoughts": "The world is so full of a number of things, I'm sure we should all be as happy as kings." The world *is* so full, and what a joy it is to experience it with our grandchildren!

Steps to Enjoying Grandparenting

1. Love and pray for your grandchildren from the day they are born.

2. Plan activities that they will enjoy. This means getting out of your comfortable ruts. Be flexible.

3. If your grandchildren live away from you, correspond with them regularly by "snail mail" (post office) or e-mail. Send pictures or packages they will enjoy. If feasible, exchange videos of interesting things you are doing.

4. Attend as many of your grandchildren's activities as possible. If you are unable to attend personally, call to express your interest and share your praise.

5. Be positive, joyful, and fun to be around.

6. Let your life be a joyous example of how the Christian faith is to be lived. Remember, we pass on the faith best by example.

Chapter 22

Make a Difference for Good

Choose this day whom you will serve.

—*Joshua 24:15*

I hadn't seen her for years, but suddenly she was sitting in front of me at a large gathering. There was no doubt about it: She still radiated peace and serenity.

Many years ago, when I moved to her city as a young minister's wife and mother of two small children, this woman was a neighbor. She was only a few years older than I, but there was something special about her even then. Usually when she stopped by my house, things were harried and I felt fragmented, yet something wonderful always happened. If I poured out my frustrations to her, she listened compassionately with her heart. If I made a big deal over trivialities, she used a light touch to remind me that this, too, would pass.

One day after a telephone conversation with my friend, I felt buoyant and full of hope. *Why?* I asked myself. *What is it about her that makes such a difference for good in the lives of others?* My conclusions that day were confirmed recently as I observed and later talked with my friend.

First and foremost, she knows "who" she is and "whose" she is. In other words, she has chosen whom she serves. As a result, she has three attributes essential to a life that makes a difference: purpose, discipline, and joy. Knowing who she is and whose she is has allowed her to exude a quiet self-confidence. Even as a young woman, she never seemed to worry about whether people liked her or not (they did because she was so likable). She didn't seem to share the concerns of many young adults about whether she and her husband were invited to the "right" parties, or whether their children had the expected developmental skills. She simply had a tremendous capacity to enjoy life each day.

Of course, I had assumed that her confidence came from a secure and trouble-free childhood. Imagine my surprise when I learned that her early life was far from idyllic. In fact, it was from the pain of her childhood experience that she developed unusual skills of sensitivity and compassion; but through it all, it was her faith that anchored her. From her grandmother, she learned early that she was made in the image of God and empowered by Christ to be all that God meant her to be. She not only learned it; she believed it with every fiber of her being. As a result, she had a confident, not arrogant, sense of self-worth.

Many people spend a lifetime looking for a purpose, haphazardly trying one thing and then another yet never feeling fulfilled. My friend instinctively seemed to know that her purpose was to be God's ambassador in relationships. In keeping with her purpose, she disciplined herself to develop interpersonal skills. For example, she took courses on marriage and parenting, communication skills, personality development, the Bible, and faith and its application in today's world. She not only took the courses, she put into action what she learned. She treasured relationships and didn't let friendships "go" by default.

As for discipline, she always was committed to keeping her body fit as well as her spirit. She followed a regime of getting up at the same early hour each morning and going to bed in time to ensure she would have eight hours of sleep. I am convinced that this helped her maintain an even disposition and allowed her time for unexpected interruptions. Her devotional life also was a top priority each morning. Perhaps it was the consistent structure of her day that caused her to appear unhurried and never frazzled.

If she sounds perfect, don't believe it. She was never perfect—just a very authentic person. If she were hurting, she shared it with a friend and expected that friend to "be there" for her. If she were irritated with her husband or children, she said so—but never acrimoniously; always with a light touch. It was her joy that made her presence feel like a spring breeze.

Knowing that she had the same trials and tribulations many of us have, I once asked her how she stayed so joyful. Her reply was, "I choose joy every day." She explained to me that joy really is a gift from God, but, as Edward FitzGerald put it in his book *Polonius* in 1852, "a gift is not a gift until you receive it."

She said that each of us has the power to choose our own thoughts, and that no one can *make* us feel anything. So each morning, instead of choosing irritation, resentment, or hostility, she said that she chose joy. She reminded me that Abraham Lincoln once said, "A man is about as happy as he makes up his mind to be." Then she added, "The same thing is true concerning joy for any man or woman."

As I looked upon my friend's face once again, I realized that her life choices are written there. Her attributes of purpose, discipline, and joy are etched on a face of serenity. She is a person who is rooted and grounded in faith; she knows who she is and whose she is. Her life is an example for all of us who want to make a difference for good.

Steps to Making a Difference for Good

1. Know who you are and whose you are.

2. Love and respect yourself. In reply to the young attorney who asked which commandment is the greatest, Jesus replied that we are to love God with every fiber of our being. Then he added: "And a second is like it: 'You shall love your neighbor as yourself'" (Matthew 22:39). Unless we love and respect ourselves, we can't love others.

3. Know your purpose for living. People without a purpose wander aimlessly through life. When I was a young person, our minister preached a sermon called "What Do You Have in Your Hand?" It was based on Exodus 4:2, where we see God asking Moses the same question. Our minister said that our talents are in our hands; and wherever they meet the needs of the world, there is where God wants us to be. That is a good criterion for people of all ages.

4. Discipline yourself. It is one thing to have a purpose or a mission and another to accomplish it. The step in between is discipline. Develop your talents, determine where those talents best "fit," and then *discipline* yourself to accomplish your purpose. In the meantime, if you are working at a job where your talents are not maximized, continue to work creatively at that job while staying focused on your

purpose and keeping your eyes open for new opportunities.

5. Choose to live each day with joy. According to Galatians 5:22, joy is a fruit of the spirit; but first we have to *choose* to allow Christ to live within us.

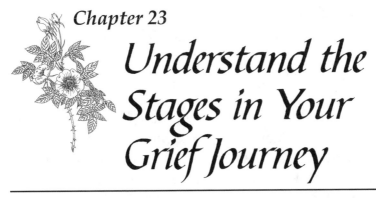

Chapter 23

Understand the Stages in Your Grief Journey

Jesus said to her, "I am the resurrection and the life. Those who believe in me, even though they die, will live, and everyone who lives and believes in me will never die. Do you believe this?"

—*John 11:25-26*

*H*e left so quickly that I didn't get to say good-bye," sobbed Olivia, my North Carolina friend whom I telephoned to express sympathy at the sudden death of her husband. John was only forty-three and was the picture of good health. Both he and Olivia played tennis several times a week, and they were health nuts when it came to nutrition.

John lived life with zest and enthusiasm. He loved Olivia and their two small children. He enjoyed his law profession and was building a good practice. He and Olivia enjoyed a wide circle of friends. And he was a man of deep Christian faith and an active church member. It was his very vibrancy that made it hard for those of us who knew him to believe that he walked into his office one Tuesday morning, put his briefcase on his desk, and fell over dead.

No wonder Olivia was so devastated by John's death. This usually decisive and competent woman became only a shadow of her former self in the months immediately following his death. She lost weight, had insomnia, was impatient with the children, and worried about their safety. In addition, she was almost paralyzed into inactivity. Her parents and friends were deeply concerned about her.

Exactly two years following John's death, I saw Olivia again. What a transformation! The sparkle was back in her eyes, her calm confidence had returned, and she was joyfully active in the lives of her children again. "What caused the change?" I asked curiously when we had time alone to talk.

"I stopped kicking against reality and allowed God to walk with me through the valley of the shadow of death. In addition to counting on and being comforted by Jesus' words, 'I will not leave you comfortless' (John 14:18 KJV), I found some very practical help through the grief recovery group at my church." Olivia told me that the wise leader of the group helped the participants move through all the stages of grief. "It is like going from Charlotte to Greensboro," the leader had said. "There are a number of towns along the way, and you can't stay permanently in any one of them if you hope to reach your destination."

The first stage the group considered was shock—the numbness that occurs when feelings are frozen; the struggle between reality and fantasy. In this stage, persons know intellectually that they have lost a loved one, but their feelings have not accepted the loss. For example, Olivia told me that she found herself listening for John's key in the lock at about six o'clock each evening. Often she found herself setting a place for him at the family dinner table, and almost every morning she awakened to reach out and touch her husband before remembering that he was not there.

In the next stage, the floodgates of real emotion open. This usually includes tears and often includes anger.

Then there is the stage of being painfully mindful of the loss when seeing old friends or going to familiar places. This stage requires real self-discipline, since the temptation is to withdraw just at the time when you need to be around people. The final stage of grief, of course, is the stage of acceptance and reaffirmation of life. Journeying through these stages is not easy, and the time required for each stage differs with individuals; but you must make the journey if you are ever to find wholeness again.

Olivia told me that the leader of her grief recovery group saw that she needed some closure to John's life since his death had been so sudden. Because Olivia had not had an opportunity to say good-bye, the leader suggested that she write her husband a letter, saying some of the things she would have said if she had been aware of his impending death. Admitting that the idea sounded a little "off the wall," Olivia nevertheless followed the suggestion. To her amazement, she found it was not primarily a sad letter about how much she missed John. Instead, it was a letter of gratitude for his vibrant life and for the positive things he had brought to her life. She was stunned to find herself writing these words: "I know that you would not want me to be immobilized by grief, causing the children to lose both a father and a mother." With that one statement, Olivia saw clearly what she must do. After all, she had lost her husband, but her children had lost their father. Immobilized by self-centered grief, she was depriving the children of both parents. That realization seemed to galvanize her out of her grief and back into life.

Though Olivia told me that her life will never be the same again and that she misses John every day, she can now say with the apostle Paul: "We know that all things work together for good for those who love God, who are called according to his purpose" (Romans 8:28).

All of us must make the grief journey. If you haven't yet, you will. In my own experience, the death of my parents and sister were hard, but not unexpected. All of them suffered for years before their lives ended, so I could honestly feel that the graduation into the eternal dimension of life was a release for each of them. It was the sudden, accidental death of our twenty-year-old son that caused me such pain. Yet I discovered two things: You have to go through each step of the grief journey before there is healing; and Jesus' promise that the Holy Spirit would walk alongside us and bring us comfort is absolutely true. You can count on it!

Steps to Take on Your Grief Journey

1. Understand that you will not escape the pain of loss in this life; it is a part of the fabric of reality. Jesus said: "In this world you will have trouble. But take heart! I have overcome the world" (John 16:33 NIV).

2. When a loss occurs, don't blame God or ask, "Why me?" Remember that when we receive blessings too numerous to count, we don't ask, "Why me?"

3. Allow yourself to experience the pain. Don't deny it or try to cover it up with busyness. Allow yourself to shed tears, temporarily withdraw, and even express anger. But don't stay in this early stage. Understand that grief is a journey, and if you stop in any one place, you never will reach your destination of wholeness and healing.

4. Don't discuss your pain with everyone you meet, but talk it out with a trusted friend, a Christian counselor, or a grief recovery group.

5. As soon as possible, resume your normal activities. Though tempted to withdraw, you need to be around people. This will take discipline on your part.

6. Keep your spiritual life alive. The Holy Spirit, which Jesus promised, will bring comfort to your mind and heart. Spend time in prayer and praise, and in regular worship.

7. Remember that you will see your loved one again. Give thanks to God for that.

Chapter 24

Never Give Up Hope

Hope does not disappoint us, because God's love has been poured into our hearts through the Holy Spirit that has been given to us.

—*Romans 5:5*

One year I was privileged to participate in the annual Celebration of Cancer Survivors' Day held in my hometown of Chattanooga. There was a luncheon cruise on the *Southern Belle* with some three hundred persons in attendance. One hundred fifty of these were actual cancer survivors. Each survivor was invited to bring a guest.

The first national Cancer Survivors' Day occurred in 1987. It was originated by Mr. and Mrs. Richard Block. Richard, a cancer survivor and cofounder of H & R Block, was appointed by President Reagan in 1982 to the National Cancer Advisory Board. It was in that position that he became acutely aware of some of the issues facing cancer survivors. Richard and his wife, Annette, established a foundation whose mission is to improve quality of life for the eight million American cancer survivors. They have accomplished this through their three books: *Fighting Cancer, There Is Hope,* and *A Guide for Cancer Supporters.* They also seek to organize, publicize, and encourage local committees to hold cancer survivor celebrations annually.

For those of us who have had cancer or those who are in the throes of it now, it is easy to think of the bad things associated with the disease—pain, nausea, hair loss, weight loss, fatigue, fear, and anxiety. *But what are some things that cancer can't do?* I asked myself as I prepared to speak to those attending the survivors' luncheon cruise.

For one thing, the disease can't keep people from enjoying the beauty of a magnificent sunrise or sunset, or the beauty in others. In Thornton Wilder's play "Our Town," Emily dies and goes to heaven. She asks permission to return to earth and relive one day, and permission is granted. She chooses her thirteenth birthday. The only restriction is that, though she can see and hear her living relatives, they are not aware of her. Her big surprise is that everyone is in such a hurry that they are insensitive to others. The most poignant lines in the play are when Emily says to her mother: "Mama, Mama, look at me. Look at me just once as if you really saw me." The lines are a poignant reminder that each day is a precious gift to be treasured. Similarly, cancer causes an individual to value every day and every relationship and never take life for granted.

Second, cancer can't make people negative. Rather, if they choose, persons can learn to count their blessings. Instead of yearning for more or concentrating on what they have lost, they can choose to look at what they have *left*. As a cancer survivor myself, I have found that priorities fall more easily into place now. I also have found that most other cancer survivors are positive, not negative; grateful, not critical. In fact, as I moved among the crowd on the cruise that day, I didn't hear a word of complaint or criticism about the food, the program, or the weather—not even the speech!

Third, cancer can't make people lose their sense of

humor. We survivors seem to know instinctively the value of laughter. We seem to know that it is like internal jogging and is good for the immune system. There certainly was nothing sad or gloomy about that survivors' cruise. Instead, gaiety, laughter, and high spirits characterized the entire afternoon.

Fourth, though cancer can destroy the body, it doesn't have to touch the spirit—the soul. And that, after all, is the real person.

In Mark 8:36, Jesus said, "What will it profit them to gain the whole world and forfeit their life?" While visiting a young mother one day, I learned how she interpreted this verse to her four-year-old daughter. Katie, the daughter, came into the room, crying. Her mother asked, "What's wrong?" and Katie sobbed, "I fell off my tricycle." Then her mother asked, "Are you hurt?" Katie replied, "I'm not hurt, but my body house is." After a little comforting, Katie went back outside. I eagerly asked the mother, "What did she mean by that answer?" Smiling, she explained:

Last year when we drove by a cemetery, Katie asked what it was. Realizing that four-year-olds don't grasp abstract ideas like immortality very easily, I simply said: "Well, we all live in body houses. Sometimes they get old or hurt and die. Then they are placed out here, but the real you goes on living forever." To illustrate this, I said, "If I pinch you, it will hurt your body house but not you; but if I say ugly or unkind things to you or hurt your feelings, it will hurt you but not your body house."

Now I understood why Katie, after her accident, had said, "I'm not hurt but my body house is."

Yes, cancer can be devastating to the body house, but it doesn't have to harm the real person. Even as I made this statement to the group of survivors on the cruise that day, I silently saluted a good friend who, that very morning, had left her body house behind as the real person moved into the eternal dimension of life. In all the years she dealt with the disease, it never once touched her spirit. Indeed, through her Christian faith, her spirit triumphed continually with positive hope, joy, and celebration of life. May that be true for each of us, no matter what difficulty or disease we may face.

Steps to Finding Hope

1. When you encounter a dead-end street in your life, look for God's options by asking, "Lord, what will you have me to do in this situation?" Remember that nothing can happen to you that you and God cannot handle. Claim and say aloud these Scripture verses: "With God all things are possible" (Matthew 19:26 NIV); "I can do all things through [Christ] who strengthens me" (Philippians 4:13).

2. In times of trouble, draw upon your spiritual equipment which includes faith, hope, and love (see 1 Corinthians 13:13).

3. Don't quit! You may be close to a breakthrough. When Florence Chadwick was practicing to swim across the English Channel, she quit one day just one-fourth mile from the shoreline. She quit because she was cold and discouraged, and because she could not see the shore through the fog. Later she commented that after that experience, whenever she swam she would keep herself going by seeing the shoreline in her mind.

4. Memorize this and other Scripture verses on

hope (note: use a Bible concordance) and use them as daily affirmations throughout the day as needed: "Hope is the anchor of the soul" (Hebrews 6:19, paraphrase).

5. Don't forget that God is your best hope!

Chapter 25

Believe in Miracles

Stephen, full of grace and power, did great wonders and signs among the people.

—*Acts 6:8*

I'll never forget a moment of panic I had some years ago. Actually, it was on a Sunday in October, at 11:21 A.M. in Charles Town, West Virginia. My husband, Ralph, and I had been in Frederick, Maryland, the day before for an all-day training event on church growth. When we had been invited to the training event, a minister from Charles Town, West Virginia, had invited us to stay over so that Ralph could preach for him. When we awakened on Sunday morning, it was one of those bright but crisp autumn days that makes you glad to be alive. The morning drive to the church was especially beautiful because the surrounding hills were covered with trees dressed in autumn gold, red, green, and purple. Not once did I imagine the challenge that awaited me.

When we arrived at the church, we were welcomed warmly by official greeters, as well as other loving laypersons. A spirit of warmth and vitality was immediately evident. The sanctuary was filled, so I was seated near the back with some people who had attended our workshop on Saturday. They were friendly, and we chatted before the prelude signaled the beginning of worship. Soon the sanctuary was filled with the sound of worshipers singing hymns the way they were meant to be sung—lustily, with feeling and joy.

Following the reading of the morning scripture by the young minister, we, as a congregation, affirmed our faith through the Apostle's Creed and prayed together the Lord's Prayer. Following the offering and Doxology, special music was presented by two instrumentalists. It was a beautiful worship service that enabled the worshipers to leave the hassles of daily living and come into the presence of Almighty God.

Then it happened! After Ralph had been introduced and began expressing appreciation for the invitation, he began to cough. At first I thought he just had a "tickle" in his throat, but it soon became apparent to me that his throat was closing up and his breathing was becoming difficult. This had happened to him only once before. That time, it had been an allergic reaction to a certain kind of flower that affected his breathing. I looked quickly at the altar and realized that the floral arrangement included the same kind of flower.

I later learned that when Ralph couldn't stop coughing and had to leave the chancel, the young minister asked in bewilderment, "What are we going to do?" Ralph gasped in reply, "Ask Nell to speak." So the minister announced to the congregation, "We are fortunate to have Mrs. Mohney with us. I would like to invite her to come and share with us." That was when terror struck! My heart began to race, my blood ran cold, my palms were sweaty, my throat went dry, and I began to tense up.

It is true that on special Sundays through the years, such as Mother's Day and Thanksgiving, I have shared the pulpit with my husband as we have presented dialogue sermons. It is also true that I have taught Sunday school for many years and have spoken to numerous groups. But in each of those situations, I have had time to plan and prepare. This time was different. Suddenly, my mind went blank. I couldn't even think of a single verse of scripture. Yet in that split second, these reassuring words flashed through my mind and immediately quieted my spirit: "The love of God surrounds you; the peace of God enfolds you; the power of God sustains you; and the grace of God goes before you." They were the four main points of a Sunday school lesson I once taught. As I calmly walked from my pew in the congregation to the pulpit, God brought to my remembrance the entire lesson. Even the scriptures and illustrations were given to me graphically and with clarity. It was a miracle!

A miracle? you wonder. Yes! A miracle, I believe, is an event that happens on a plane higher than our understanding. As a result, miracles occur all around us, but we are usually too preoccupied with what comes next to see them. I shall never doubt that this particular incident in my life was a miracle, and I shall never stop being grateful for it.

As I have reflected on the incident, several things seem clear to me. First, this is not the kind of thing God does Sunday after Sunday. Once I heard a lazy preacher whose sermons were very unappealing say, "I never prepare. I just stand up and wait for the Holy Spirit to tell me what to say." This, I believe, is an affront to God. God has given us minds and expects us to use them.

Second, when we do our work faithfully each day, God has more resources with which to help us in a crisis. It was because I had carefully prepared a lesson years earlier that God could "bring it to my remembrance."

Third, it was God, and certainly not I, who performed the miracle and rescued me from helplessness. We need to remember that we can trust God completely because always God's love surrounds us, God's peace enfolds us, God's power sustains us, and God's grace goes before us. Thanks be to God!

Steps to Enable You to Believe in Miracles

1. Recognize that a miracle is an event that happens on a plane higher than your understanding and, as a result, miracles occur all around you. Do not be too preoccupied with what comes next to see them!

2. Ask yourself: "Does this mean that I should throw away my logic in order to see miracles?" Absolutely not! God has given us minds and expects us to use them to discover truth. Remember that all truth comes from God. Jesus said: "You will know the truth, and the truth will make you free" (John 8:32).

3. Continue to study and learn in all disciplines of life—especially the spiritual. This means cultivating a growing knowledge of the Word of God through disciplined study. It also means staying in close relationship, through prayer, with the One who said, "I am the way, and the truth, and the life" (John 14:6).

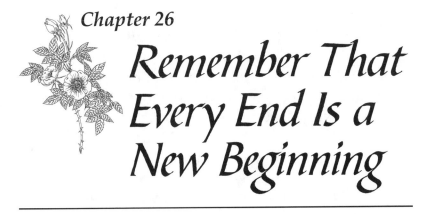

Chapter 26

Remember That Every End Is a New Beginning

In all these things we are more than conquerors through him who loved us.

—Romans 8:37

*J*enny burst into my office without even knocking. Fortunately, no one was with me, because nothing could have stopped her from blurting out: "My husband has been having an affair with my best friend, and I hate them both!"

There was no doubt about it: Jenny was at the end of her rope. She felt that her marriage—and life as she knew it—was coming to an end. Though we may not have walked in Jenny's shoes, all of us have experienced or will experience what seem to be hopeless situations in life—disappointments, broken relationships, unexpected illnesses or accidents, natural disasters, financial reverses, the death of loved ones, and many other difficult circumstances. The question is, What do we do then?

I'm convinced that Jenny was taking the right first step by allowing herself to feel the pain and process that pain by talking with a trusted friend or counselor. This important step, however, doesn't involve talking with everyone or bogging down in resentment.

The second step is to look honestly and objectively at the situation. Jenny learned that the "affair" was a one-night indiscretion, which happened early in their marriage. In those days, Jenny had often been upset about something and had gone home to her mother for weeks at a time. Now, fifteen years later, theirs was a much more mature relationship, and she knew in her heart that Tim loved her. By seeing a Christian counselor, they were able to work through the pain, experience forgiveness, and renew their marriage vows. By recognizing and working on areas in which they each needed help, their relationship became stronger than ever.

The third step, then, is to move on. The Twenty-third Psalm gives some practical advice here. The fourth verse reads: "Yea, though I walk through the valley of the shadow of death, I will fear no evil: for thou art with me; thy rod and thy staff they comfort me" (KJV). It does not suggest that we stay in the valley or try to go back to the mountain where we were. Instead, the psalmist instructs us to go through the difficult experience and to move forward, knowing that God is with us.

Several years ago on a speaking engagement in North Carolina, I decided to leave the hotel lobby and walk outside into the early spring sunshine to await my ride. On a ledge nearby was a steadily moving ant. The Bible mentions the ant several times, indicating that it is wise, industrious, resourceful, and highly organized socially. So, that morning I decided to give the ant a test by putting some problems or obstacles in its way.

First, I built a hill in the sand. The ant never broke stride but walked up one side of the hill and down the other. Then I placed a small rock in front of him. He tried to climb over, struggled a bit, fell back, reconsidered, and went around the rock. My final test was a rather large twig. Once again he struggled, but finally he walked over it, dealing with its ups and downs. Amid all the obstacles, the ant never quit. He kept moving, though several times he stopped long enough to reconsider his plan of action. He didn't complain or go to the ant colony to solve his problems.

Jenny and Tim followed much of the same procedure. They struggled, fell back, reconsidered their options, and moved ahead. They remembered that the Chinese characters for the word *crisis* mean "trouble" *and* "opportunity." Most of all, they learned the truth of this statement by Phillips Brooks, perhaps one of the best preachers of the nineteenth century: "Life is full of ends, but every end is a new beginning." Or as Julius Rosenwald, former president of Sears Roebuck, once said, "When life gives you a lemon, make lemonade."

Steps to Finding New Beginnings

1. Remember that most people don't go far in life without encountering detours. Life has a way of saying "no" to us.
2. Remember, also, that life is not fair, but God is good; and God will never leave you nor forsake you.
3. When your detour comes, find an alternate route. Take time to evaluate your situation and look for new possibilities.
4. Don't bog down in resentment and self-pity. It is self-destructive and will cause you to put your life on hold. You will stay focused on the detour rather than on the alternate route.
5. Try to be objective as you evaluate. You will be tempted to blame others without asking if you

---

helped to bring on the situation. You may need the help of a counselor to sort this out.

6. Always seek God's guidance—not only about the alternate route, but also about what God wants you to learn from the situation.

7. Repeat this affirmation: "Give thanks in all circumstances; for this is the will of God in Christ Jesus for you" (1 Thessalonians 5:18). I believe the apostle Paul didn't mean that we are to give thanks for the problem, but that in the midst of it we are to give thanks. In other words, we don't focus on what we have lost, but on what we have left. Only then can we see the new beginning.